Mon Égal à toi.
Couleur n'est rien, le cœur est tout ;
n'est tu pas mon frère ?

Endsheets:

**SHANGO QUILT, CIRCA 1830,
COTTON, ARKANSAS**

*Made by an enslaved craftswoman, the
quilt and its distinctive African motif honor
Shango, a religious deity who is often invoked by
believers for his influence on male potency and
fertility.*

Frontispiece:

MOI EGAL À TOI
Artist: F. Bonneville.

Preceding pages:

**FREED SLAVES, 1862,
SOUTH CAROLINA**

*A group of freed slaves gather on the plantation
of Confederate General Thomas F. Drayton in
Hilton Head, South Carolina, during Union
occupation of the property.*

Following pages:

FAMILY MIGRATION, 1910
*A family from the rural South arrives in Chicago
to look for new economic opportunities.*

One of the world's largest non-
profit scientific and educational
organizations, the NATIONAL
GEOGRAPHIC SOCIETY was
founded in 1888 "for the
increase and diffusion of geographic knowledge."
Fulfilling this mission, the Society educates and
inspires millions every day through its magazines,
books, television programs, videos, maps and atlases,
research grants, the National Geographic Bee,
teacher workshops, and innovative classroom materials. The Society is supported through membership
dues, charitable gifts, and income from the sale of
its educational products. This support is vital to
National Geographic's mission to increase global
understanding and promote conservation of our
planet through exploration, research, and education.

For more information, please call
1-800-NGS LINE (647-5463) or
write to the following address:
NATIONAL GEOGRAPHIC SOCIETY
1145 17th Street N.W.
Washington, D.C. 20036-4688 U.S.A.

Visit the Society's Web site at
www.nationalgeographic.com.

Published by the National Geographic Society,
1145 17th Street N.W., Washington, D.C.
20036

First printing 2002
Copyright © 2002 The New York Public
Library, Astor, Lenox and Tilden Foundations
Additional copyright information can be found
on page 224.

The names "The New York Public Library" and
the "Schomburg Center for Research in Black
Culture" are registered marks and the property of
The New York Public Library, Astor, Lenox and
Tilden Foundations.

Printed in Spain

Library of Congress Cataloging-in-Publication Data

Dodson, Howard.
   Jubilee : the emergence of African American culture / Schomburg Center for Research
in Black Culture, New York Public Library; text by Howard Dodson ; with Amiri
Baraka ... [et al.].
      p. cm.
   Includes bibiographical references and index.
   ISBN 0-7922-6982-9 (hc)
      1. African Americans--History. 2. African Americans--Social life and customs.
3. African Americans--Intellectual life. 4. Blacks--America--History. 5. Blacks--America--
Social life and customs. 6. Blacks--America--Intellectual life. 7. United States--
Civilization--African American influences. 8. America--Civilization--African influences.
I. Schomburg Center for Research in Black Culture. II. Title.

E185 .D63 2003
305.896'073--dc21

                                                                                    2002024504

JUBILEE

THE EMERGENCE OF AFRICAN-AMERICAN CULTURE

SCHOMBURG CENTER FOR RESEARCH IN BLACK CULTURE
THE NEW YORK PUBLIC LIBRARY

BY HOWARD DODSON

WITH AMIRI BARAKA, GAIL BUCKLEY, JOHN HOPE FRANKLIN, HENRY LOUIS GATES, JR.,
ANNETTE GORDON-REED, AND GAYRAUD S. WILMORE

NATIONAL GEOGRAPHIC

WASHINGTON, D.C.

CONTENTS

PORTRAIT OF A WOMAN, 1880, BAHIA, BRAZIL

More than 3.5 million slaves were imported to Brazil during the slavery era, more than to any colony in the Americas. Although the slave trade had been officially outlawed in Brazil in 1831, tens of thousands of slaves continued to be imported over the next 50 years. On May 13, 1888, Brazil became the last nation in the Western Hemisphere to abolish slavery. In 1890 all official papers and documents relating to the Brazilian slave trade were ordered burned. Today, only Nigeria has a larger black population than Brazil.

FOREWORD

by WYNTON MARSALIS

Growing up in New Orleans, I was never far away from the legacies of American slavery. Being a member of the post-civil-rights generation, I tended to look upon the pre-civil-rights heritage as something to be ashamed of; and it was not until I moved to New York City in my late teens that I began to understand the value of the spiritual and cultural inheritance from slavery. From my childhood, I remember the many parades and social functions that were drenched in African and Afro-Americanism. From this perspective, I could see just how much of the old ways carry on. In 1817 the city council had designated Congo Square as a place where enslaved Africans could gather and practice their religious and cultural heritage. As many as 20 distinct African national or ethnic groups would gather to dance and sing in traditional ways, dressed in traditional African garb, playing slave-made replicas of traditional African drums. Over the decades leading up to the Civil War these weekly rituals continued. Our enslaved African forebears, drawing on their varied customs, began to create new forms of American music and dance, and new *African-American* cultural forms emerged from a synthesis of the African and European life in New Orleans.

What *Jubilee*, a much needed edition, tells us is that the enslaved Africans were truly remarkable people. How else do you explain the fact that enslaved African human beings, living under the most oppressive and exploitative conditions imaginable, still managed to reinvent themselves, reclaim their humanity, and not just survive slavery but create fresh and vibrant responses to American democracy. Inventing as they did, in the midst of slavery, new languages, new religions, new art forms, new families, and new lifestyles—they were miraculous.

Jubilee: The Emergence of African-American Culture offers a fresh look at slavery—perhaps the most defining issue in our nation's history. Beyond the victimization that is the singular achievement of slavery, *Jubilee* reveals the self-actualizing, creative, and self-determining acts of enslaved Africans that transformed them and our nation. Every American needs to read *Jubilee*. Read it and celebrate the triumph of the human spirit.

MA RAINEY AND HER GEORGIA JAZZ BAND, GRAND THEATRE, CHICAGO, 1923
Gertrude Pridgett "Ma" Rainey (1886-1939) was the daughter of minstrel performers Thomas and Ella Pridgett. Married to showman William "Pa" Rainey, the "mother of the blues" later toured as a soloist with the Rabbit Foot Minstrels, where she cultivated her classic blues style before first recording in Chicago in 1923.

INTRODUCTION

by **HOWARD DODSON,** Director, Schomburg Center for Research in Black Culture

Jubilee: The Emergence of African-American Culture presents a new perspective on slavery and the slave trade. Unlike many previous accounts, it does not focus on blacks as victims. Rather, it focuses on the cultural, political, economic, and social activities that enslaved Africans took in the midst of slavery to redefine themselves and their world and reshape their own destinies. It is the story of the ways in which enslaved African human beings made themselves history- and culture-makers and transformed themselves.

Drawing on the most recent scholarship on slavery and the slave trade, *Jubilee* offers the American public—black as well as white—a unique opportunity to discover a compelling history of the American past—facts that, until recently, have been unavailable to the public for study and reflection. Of the first 6.5 million people who crossed the Atlantic and settled in the Americas during the colonial period (1492-1776), for instance, only 1 million were Europeans. The other 5.5 million were African. Equally intriguing is the fact that only some 450,000 of the 10 million Africans who survived the Middle Passage during the transatlantic slave trade settled in the continental United States. Nevertheless, these 450,000 had grown to more than 4 million people of African descent by 1860, and more than 40 million today.

For more than two centuries, slavery was a central factor in the development of American life. The transatlantic slave trade's more than 300-year history shaped the modern world as we know it. It fueled the economic development of Europe, disrupted Africa's economic and political and social life, and provided the labor force that laid the economic foundation of the Americas, including the United States. Together, the slave trade and slavery were the two most powerful forces shaping the development of the American nation. Nevertheless, the vast majority of Americans—black and white—know very little about the nature and character of these people-shaping, nation-building institutions.

Most Americans have avoided any serious study of these institutions. Whites have shied away from any earnest attempts to really know what

THE BUILDERS, 1974

Silkscreen print. Artist: Jacob Lawrence
At the age of 13, Jacob Lawrence (1917-2000) moved with his family from Philadelphia to Harlem. During the 1930s he studied under Charles Alston and worked at the Harlem Arts Project (sponsored by the Works Progress Administration). Famed for his narrative series depicting black historical events and figures (Toussaint L'Ouverture, Frederick Douglass, and Harriet Tubman), Lawrence called his vibrant and vivid style of painting "dynamic cubism."

happened during slavery because they fear that they will be implicated in its horrors. They fear that they will find their ancestors' behavior and actions repugnant and that they will be obliged to shoulder the burden of guilt. Blacks avoid such study because they fear that they will be further demeaned or embarrassed by such knowledge. Much of this fear and avoidance stems from the images of slavery and the slave trade that most Americans have come to believe are the essence of slavery and the slave trade's history and legacy.

What Americans know or think they know about slavery and the slave trade has been shaped by the images of these institutions that have been handed down to us over the past 500 years. They are images of helpless, defenseless victims of unthinkable cruelty. They are images of long lines of bound captives being driven by armed captors from the interior of West and Central Africa to coastal holding pens.

They are images of hundreds and at times thousands of these enslaved African captives being held in jail cells and other prisonlike settings until enough have been captured to fill a slave ship. They are images of men, women, and children in shackles and leg irons. They are images of hundreds of these African men, women, and children packed spoon-fashion on slave ships. They are images of brutalized, exploited slaves working under unbearable conditions on tobacco and cotton plantations in the United States and sugar plantations throughout the Americas. They are images of downtrodden, degraded people—perennial victims—who were stripped of their culture and humanity and forced to live out their lives in slavery as pawns in vicious, all-powerful systems of human degradation.

Ironically, most of these images of slavery were fashioned and promulgated during the heat of the abolitionist struggle against slavery prior to the Civil War. Fugitive slaves, free blacks, and abolitionists alike created and focused public attention on such iconic images in order to hasten the destruction of the slave trade and slavery. To counter the slaveholders' perspective, which painted benign, paternalistic images of the "peculiar institution," slavery's opponents documented and presented for public consumption every instance of brutality and victimization in the slave-holding South. Seeking to appeal to the moral consciousness and sensibilities of ordinary citizens, churches, governments and principalities of power, abolitionists and anti-slavery proponents created graphic visual and narrative pictures of the brutal and dehumanizing nature of the slave trade and slavery. More critiques of the behavior of the slave traders, masters, and overseers than accurate por-trayals of slavery in the lives and culture of the enslaved African captives, they were nonetheless effective resources in the propaganda war between the proponents of slavery and abolition that preceded the Civil War.

This almost singular focus on black victimization has, until recently, dominated scholarship and public thinking about the slave trade and slavery. Over the past three decades, however, scholars have posed a variety of new questions about the nature and functioning of both institutions. The slave trade has come to be seen as more than a set of oppressive relations between villainous slave-ship captains and crews and cowering African victims. And slavery is now understood to be more than a cruel history of day-to-day acts of brutality and unrequited labor.

The slave trade and slavery laid the foundations for the development of Europe and the Americas as well as the underdevelopment of Africa from the 16th through the 19th centuries. Of even greater significance, as *Jubilee* makes clear, is that it was in the context of slavery that enslaved Africans invented and reproduced themselves and laid the foundations of African-American social, political, cultural, and economic development. Though victimized, exploited, and oppressed, enslaved Africans and their progeny— both slave and free—were active, creative agents in the making of their own history, culture, and political future.

Studying their lives can teach us much about the capacity of human beings to develop even under dehumanizing conditions. It can teach us some of the diverse ways in which oppressed human beings confront and tran-scend oppression. It can teach us about living, surviving, and winning in the face of seemingly insurmountable odds. *Jubilee* documents and interprets

**PORTRAIT OF A WOMAN, CIRCA 1880,
BAHIA, BRAZIL**
*A woman in traditional clothes sells fruit from
her basket. Albumen print.*

these obstacle-ridden but life-affirming experiences of enslaved African peoples in the Americas, especially in the United States.

Jubilee is divided into three parts. Part One traces the origin and development of the slave trade and slavery. Using graphic visual images and selected narrative documents, it describes and interprets the context in which enslaved Africans remade themselves and their world. Part Two documents the processes of social, cultural, political, and economic change that enslaved Africans fashioned in order to create and affirm their new identities and humanity. Chapters within this part explore the transformations wrought by enslaved Africans in such areas as language, religion, family life, expressive culture, and politics. Part Three relates how Abraham Lincoln's presidential decree, the Emancipation Proclamation, placed the U.S. government on the side of freedom. Essays by distinguished authorities complement the visual and textual narratives that compose the heart of each chapter.

The Schomburg Center is pleased to join forces with National Geographic to present this book. *Jubilee: The Emergence of African-American Culture* is based on an exhibition organized by the Schomburg Center as part of its 75th-anniversary celebration in 2000-2001. Most of the objects presented here are drawn from the collections of the Schomburg Center. Collectors Sample Pittman, Danny Drain, Eugene and Adele Redd, and Gene Alexander Peters contributed to the success of the exhibit and this publication by lending items from their collections. Artists Rod Brown and Tom Feelings also loaned artworks on slavery and the slave trade. To all who participated, I extend my thanks and appreciation.

ENSLAVEMENT

The King of Dahomy

CHAPTER 1

THE TRANSATLANTIC SLAVE TRADE

Between 1500 and the 1870s millions of Africans were captured and enslaved on the African continent and transported across the Atlantic Ocean to the Americas, where they became the dominant workforce in Euro-American colonial economies. Slavery as a system of labor organization and exploitation had developed in antiquity. Ancient Egypt, Greece and Rome, ancient China, as well as the Inca and the Aztec cultures of the pre-colonial Americas, were all slave societies. Slavery on the rest of the African continent dated back to ancient times as well and was still a part of the social structure of most African societies when the Europeans came.

Native Americans were among the first slaves of European colonists in the Americas. When the Native American slave population began to succumb to European diseases and the rigorous work routine, a Spanish Dominican priest proposed to the King of Spain that Africans be substituted for the Native American slaves. (The first shipload of enslaved Africans in the transatlantic slave trade, carried to Saint Domingue [Haiti] in 1503, had proved themselves capable of surviving the diseases and the labor.) In 1510 the King of Spain finally launched the transatlantic slave trade, when he ordered that 50 slaves be sent to Haiti to replace Native Americans in the gold mines. It was the Portuguese, however, who dominated the first two centuries of the trade. Between 1500 and 1700 they established trading bases in West Africa, principally in the Congo-Angola region. Over these first two centuries of the trade, some 1.7 million enslaved Africans were taken to the Americas, principally to Brazil and the Caribbean.

The majority of the captives continued to come from the west-central African regions of Congo-Angola, followed by enslaved Africans from the Bight of Benin, the Bight of Biafra, the Gold Coast, Senegambia, and upper Guinea. Another 3.5 million arrived in the Americas during the 19th century. The vast majority of the captives who survived were young men and boys age 14 to 30. Young girls and women age 14 to 30 were 25 percent of the total. Slave ships from Massachusetts sailed to Africa in 1638. They were the first to enter the trade from the North American colonies, but by 1770,

Previous pages:

GORÉE ISLAND, SENEGAL

Gorée Island became the headquarters for England's slave-trading operations in Africa in the 1660s. Located on the Gold Coast, it exported African captives for more than 200 years. Every country in Europe sought to establish trading ports along the coast of Africa; the forts were built not to defend slave traders' holdings from Africans but from other Europeans. Prior to embarking on board ship, enslaved Africans were held within the forts' dungeons.

Opposite:

KING TEGESIBU OF DAHOMEY, WEST AFRICA

During the 1750s King Tegesibu sold more than 9,000 slaves a year, making upward of £250,000 a year for selling African captives into slavery. King Agaja, his father, established slave trading as the principal business of the kingdom.

AFRICAN SQUADRON, 1842

Despite the Act of 1807 abolishing the slave trade and the vigorous efforts of Britain's African Squadron, the trade continued well into the 1870s.

Rhode Island, the smallest American colony, commanded 70 percent of the North American trade. Between 1709 and 1807, when the slave trade in the United States was officially abolished, 934 ships from Rhode Island carried 106,544 African captives into bondage. Bristol, Rhode Island; Charleston, South Carolina; Providence, Rhode Island; Boston and Salem, Massachusetts; and New York City were the leading slave-trading centers in the United States. New York ships made 151 slaving voyages to Africa between 1715 and 1774. Between 1792 and 1807, Charleston merchants sent 110 ships to Africa to buy and import slaves to strengthen its and the nation's cotton-plantation economy. Within the overall context of the transatlantic slave trade, however, the United States and the North American colonies were relatively minor players. Only 450,000 of the more than 10 million African voyagers who survived ended up within the continental limits of today's United States.

The transatlantic slave trade was central to the development of the European colonial economies in the Americas from the 16th to the 19th centuries. Indeed, it was central to the development of the modern world as we know it. The transatlantic slave trade established economic, political, social, and cultural relations among peoples in Africa, Europe, and the Americas that eventually transformed the nature of the Atlantic world. Prior to the trade, Europe, Africa, and the Americas lived in relative isolation from one another. The trade molded them into an interdependent Atlantic economy. Economic and political elite on four continents and in the Caribbean entered into alliances that made the slave trade a profitable economic enterprise. The trade, in turn, fostered the material development of elite in Europe and Africa as well as European colonial elite in North, Central, and South America and the Caribbean.

Frequently referred to as the "triangular trade," the slave trade linked the economies of four continents and the Caribbean into an Atlantic world economy. Spain, Portugal, the Netherlands, England, and France dominated the trade. Trading activities took place in three stages. Ships left ports along the western European seaboard laden with trade goods bound for Africa. Arriving in Africa, ship captains traded their goods for captive Africans. Firearms and gunpowder came to dominate the trade, but textiles, beads, other manufactured goods, and rum also figured prominently in it. The process of trading goods for captives on the coast of Africa could last from a week to months. The second leg of the triangular trade, the "Middle Passage," transported shiploads of captured Africans across the Atlantic for sale in the Americas.

African Squadron

UNPARALLELED SUCCESS.

" The *Bonnetta* has been 2 years and 11 months in commission, and is now ordered to be paid off at Chatham. The Commander, Lieutenant FORBES, has been employed during the past year in negociating with the King of Dahomey, in the endeavour to establish a Treaty for the **Abolition of the Slave Trade** throughout his territory, **but which failed. His Majesty** reviewed his Troops during Commander FORBES' sojourn with him, and they are spoken of as well disciplined, though 4000 out of 10,000 of the Soldiery are Women, clothed as Men, who perform in every respect as well as their male companions in Arms*. His Majesty, as a **mark of His especial favour,** presented Commander FORBES with a **Juvenile Princess.** At the '**Customs**' (a **sort** of **Religious** rite), **30 Human Sacrifices** were offered to their Deity; two of these (soldiers from Attapahme,) Commander FORBES **purchased for 100 dollars,** and sent to Fernando Po to be liberated.

THE SLAVE TRADE WAS VERY BRISK."

(Portsmouth Paper.)

This is in the 35th year since the Act for the Abolition of the Slave Trade passed, and after Eighty Millions of money have been spent.

These are the Majesties Queen Victoria's name is degraded by being brought into contact with.

des Schiffes

es

des Schiffes

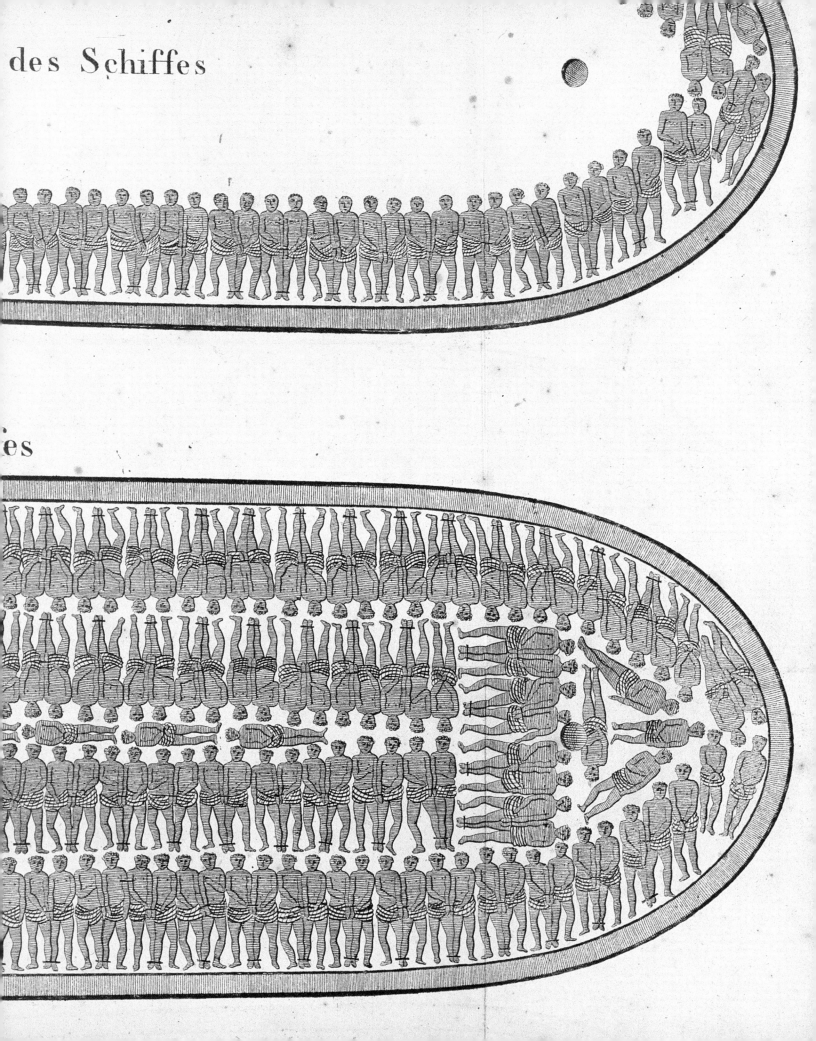

The final stage of the triangular trade ran from the Americas to Europe. Ships carried goods—principally agricultural products grown with slave labor—to European ports, where they fueled the development of European manufactures. Sugar dominated, followed by cotton, coffee, tobacco, and rice. In the early years, Spanish and Portuguese ships carried gold and silver from American mines—mines worked by African and Native American labor. Direct trade between metropolitan European countries and their American colonies was also dependent on slavery, especially in the 17th and 18th centuries.

Kings, queens, princes, and nation-states licensed individuals and companies to enter the slave trade, charged taxes on their enterprises, and collected duties on goods sold. They also formed and played leadership roles in the establishment of state-owned, -endorsed, or -sponsored slave-trading companies, such as the British Royal African Company and the Dutch West India Company, and shared in the profits of each successful voyage. The major owners, investors, or supporters of slave-trade enterprises ranged from Louis XIV of France and María Cristina, Queen Mother of Spain, to King Tegesibu of Dahomey and King Don Alvare of the Congo. Popes Eugenius IV, Nicholas V, and Calixtus III all endorsed or sanctioned exclusive rights to control the slave trade. The governor of the Bank of England, the mayor of Liverpool, the director of the Bank of Bahia, and the future president of the Continental Congress of the United States were owners, directors, and/or stockholders in slave-trading companies.

The slave-ship captains were often people who aspired to higher status. The profits made in the trade frequently elevated them to elite status in their respective societies and rewarded them with high positions and offices. John Newton became the vicar of St. Mary's Church. James de Wolf became a U.S. senator. Esek Hopkins became the commander of the U.S. Navy, and Joseph Wanton, the governor of Rhode Island.

The profits made on slaving voyages that reached their destinations with a healthy slave cargo were enormous. A simple round-trip voyage from Havana, Cuba, to the African coast and back to Havana netted its owner a $41,000 profit on a $39,000 investment. It had transported and sold 217 enslaved Africans. Another ship carrying 250 enslaved men and 100 enslaved girls and boys netted $190,000. Slave-trade voyages that included all three legs of the triangle were even more profitable. An estimated 36,000 slave-trading voyages transported the 10 million Africans who survived the Middle Passage.

DESCRIPTION OF A SLAVE SHIP, 1789

This engraving shows a cross section of the slave ship Brookes, *based in Liverpool. British member of Parliament William Wilberforce used the diagram in arguments before the House of Commons for the abolition of the slave trade in 1807. Published in England in 1789, the engraving was later published in other European countries.*

RENAISSANCE AND ROYALTY

Louis XIV of France

Pope Pius II

Ironically, the riches that financed the Renaissance of fine art, architecture, music, and literature in Europe came largely from profits from slave labor and the international slave trade. "A ship full of blacks brings more to the Treasury than galleons and fleets put together," proclaimed Pedro Zapata de Mendoza, governor of modern-day Colombia, in 1648.

HENRY THE NAVIGATOR (1394-1460), the founder of the Portuguese Colonial Empire, encouraged sailors and merchants to invest in the African slave trade. A pioneer in the transatlantic slave trade, Prince Henry spearheaded the development of enslaved Africans as marketable commodities. **POPE PIUS II** (1405-1464) opposed the enslavement of Africans who had converted to Christianity but never condemned the slave trade or slavery itself. His predecessors, Popes Eugenius IV, Nicholas V, and Calixtus III, had granted Prince Henry and Portugal exclusive rights over her African discoveries, including the slave trade. Portugal's chief African trading partner, **KING DON ÁLVARE** (circa 1540-1587) of the Congo, is said to have used 400,000 slaves as soldiers to strengthen his kingdom. King Álvare commonly sold as many as 3,000 slaves in a single market.

In the 17th century England's **KING CHARLES II** (1630-1685) created the Royal Adventurers, a slave-trading enterprise (later known as the Royal African Company) and gave the new company a "thousand years" monopoly on the English-African slave trade. He appointed his brother, **JAMES II, DUKE OF YORK** (1633-1701), as president. In 1664 the English navy captured New Netherlands from the Dutch and the colony was renamed New York, after the duke, who immediately granted port privileges and warehouse priorities in the colony to ships engaged in the slave trade.

To encourage the use of slave labor in French colonies, **KING LOUIS XIV OF FRANCE** (1643-1715) established the practice of paying a bounty for every slave delivered live to the Americas. He and his grandson, Philip V, also owned half the stock in the Guinea Company, to which he awarded the prized asiento in 1702. Reputedly the "richest individual in Europe," the queen mother of Spain, **MARÍA CRISTINA DE BORBÓN** (1806-1878), profited heavily from the Cuban slave and sugar trade.

Henry the Navigator

James II, Duke of York

*María Cristina
of Spain*

26

SLAVE-TRADE MERCHANTS

Many highly respected merchants, bankers, and politicians on both sides of the Atlantic were engaged in the slave trade. Throughout Europe and the Americas, thousands of individual investors, perhaps knowingly or unknowingly, profited from slavery and slavery-related enterprises, including investments in copper, silver, and gold mining, lumber, tobacco, cotton, and sugar.

HUMPHREY MORICE (1679-1731) was a member of Parliament and governor of the Bank of England from 1727 to 1728. In 1720 he owned eight ships engaged in the slave trade, all named after his wife and daughters. **THOMAS GOLIGHTLY** (1732-1821), mayor of Liverpool, England, traded in slaves until the trade was abolished in 1807. Like other prominent English merchants, **CHARLES GOORE** (1701-1783) profited from a diverse portfolio, which included Virginia tobacco and slaves. **HENRY LAURENS** (1724-1792) and George Austin of Charleston, South Carolina, began to trade slaves in 1748. The firm of Austin and Laurens traded wine, beer, rice, indigo, and indentured servants, as well as slaves, but by 1755 carried about a quarter of Charleston's slaving business—700 slaves a year. Laurens made 10 percent profit on every slave imported. He later entered politics and, at the commencement of the American Revolution, became president of the Continental Congress. **ANTOINE WALSH** (1703-1763), an Irish Catholic immigrant in France, sent 57 slave-trading expeditions to Africa. In 1749 he established a slave-trading enterprise, Société d'Angola, sending 10,000 slaves to Saint Domingue and elsewhere in the Caribbean. **JOAQUIN PEREIRA MARINHO** (1782-1854), of Bahia, Brazil, was a director of both the Joazeiro Railway and the Bank of Bahia and a leader in the illegal slave trade after it was abolished. He sent 36 voyages to Africa from Bahia and was responsible for half of the slaving voyages to Bahia between 1842 and 1851. He became a Portuguese baron, viscount, and count. **JULIAN ZULUETA** (1814-1878), of Havana, Cuba, was the chief stockholder in the company "Expedición por Africa," which owned 20 ships. Zulueta probably brought in most of the 100,000 slaves imported into Cuba between 1858 and 1862.

Humphrey Morice

Charles Goore

Joaquin Pereira Marinho

Julian Zulueta

Thomas Golightly

Antoine Walsh

Henry Laurens

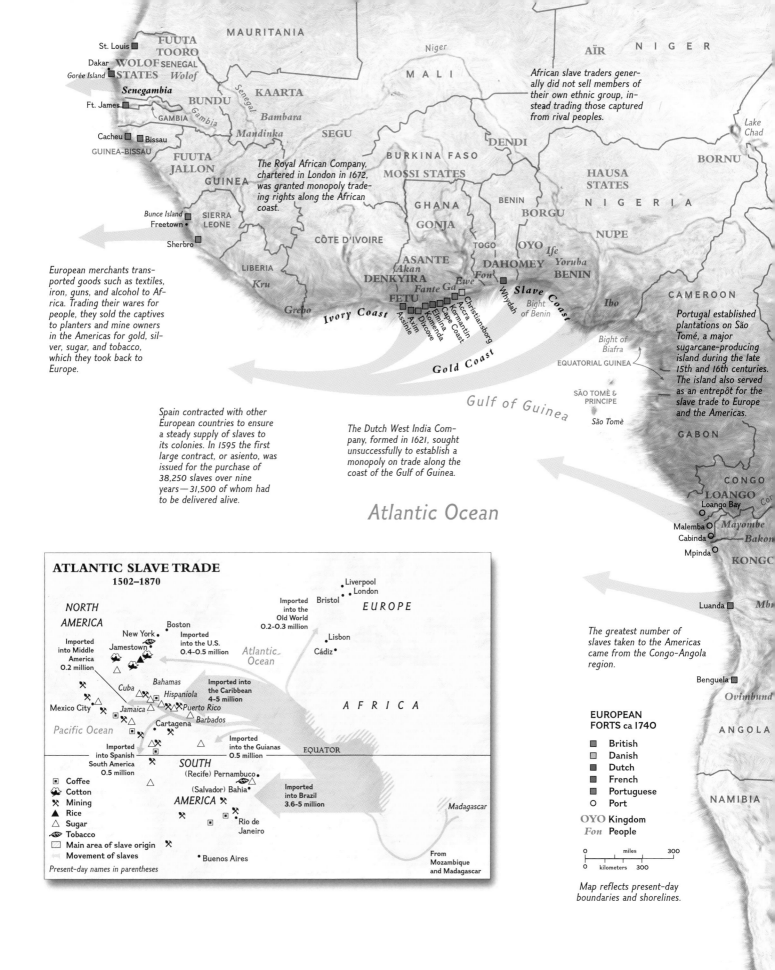

African slave traders generally did not sell members of their own ethnic group, instead trading those captured from rival peoples.

The Royal African Company, chartered in London in 1672, was granted monopoly trading rights along the African coast.

European merchants transported goods such as textiles, iron, guns, and alcohol to Africa. Trading their wares for people, they sold the captives to planters and mine owners in the Americas for gold, silver, sugar, and tobacco, which they took back to Europe.

Spain contracted with other European countries to ensure a steady supply of slaves to its colonies. In 1595 the first large contract, or asiento, was issued for the purchase of 38,250 slaves over nine years—31,500 of whom had to be delivered alive.

The Dutch West India Company, formed in 1621, sought unsuccessfully to establish a monopoly on trade along the coast of the Gulf of Guinea.

Portugal established plantations on São Tomé, a major sugarcane-producing island during the late 15th and 16th centuries. The island also served as an entrepôt for the slave trade to Europe and the Americas.

The greatest number of slaves taken to the Americas came from the Congo-Angola region.

ATLANTIC SLAVE TRADE
1502–1870

Imported into the Old World 0.2–0.3 million

Imported into the U.S. 0.4–0.5 million

Imported into Middle America 0.2 million

Imported into the Caribbean 4–5 million

Imported into Spanish South America 0.5 million

Imported into the Guianas 0.5 million

Imported into Brazil 3.6–5 million

From Mozambique and Madagascar

- ⊡ Coffee
- 🐚 Cotton
- ⚒ Mining
- ▲ Rice
- △ Sugar
- 🐚 Tobacco
- ☐ Main area of slave origin
- ⟵ Movement of slaves

Present-day names in parentheses

EUROPEAN FORTS ca 1740

- ■ British
- ▫ Danish
- ■ Dutch
- ■ French
- ■ Portuguese
- ○ Port

OYO Kingdom
Fon People

Map reflects present-day boundaries and shorelines.

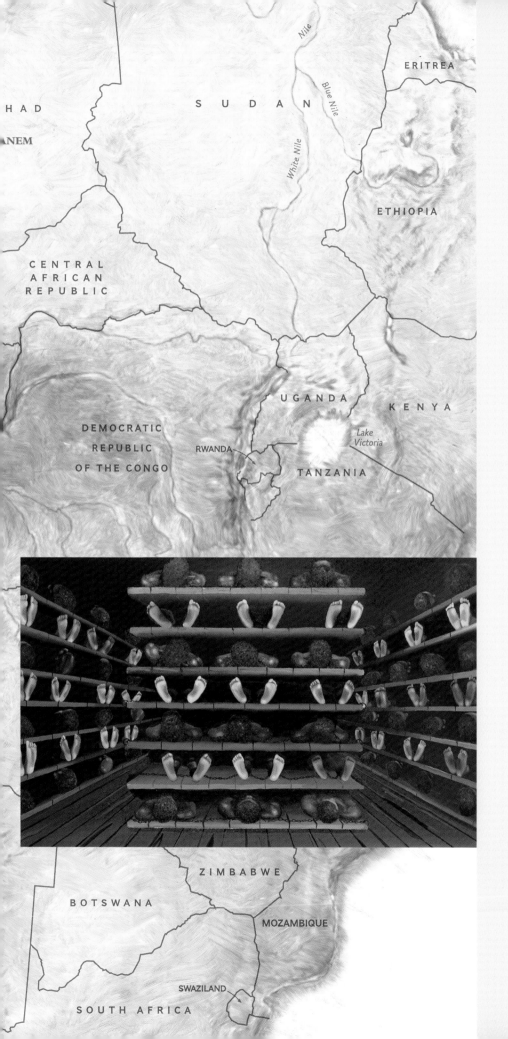

AFRICA'S LIVING TREASURE

By conservative estimates upward of 10 million Africans survived the Middle Passage and were enslaved in the Americas. More than 90 percent of these Africans were taken to South America and the Caribbean Islands. About 4.6 percent, or roughly half a million Africans, were transported to the United States. Nearly twice as many were sent to Cuba (7.3 percent), Jamaica (7.8 percent), and Haiti (9 percent). The majority of enslaved Africans, about five million, were transported to South America, most to Brazil (38.2 percent).

Africa: The Long March

European political, commercial, and business interests organized and managed the European and American dimensions of the slave trade. Slave ships were manufactured and fitted out in European and American ports. These ships, manned by European and American captains and crews, transported enslaved Africans from Africa to the Americas. European and American finance capital paid for the ships, the slave cargo, and the costs of transport. European and American traders sold the slave cargo in the Americas and employed them as slave laborers in plantation, mining, and other economies. European and American companies transformed slave-produced agricultural products into manufactured goods to be sold as consumer goods in Europe or traded in Africa for slaves. Urban and national European economies were organized around the slave trade. They were controlled by Europeans, as were the plantation economies organized by European colonials and American colonialists. The one sector of the trade that the Europeans never gained control of was the procurement of enslaved African labor on the African continent.

The European presence in Africa during the era of the slave trade was largely limited to a series of forts, slave castles, and trading posts along the coast. When the transatlantic slave trade started during the 16th century, Portuguese traders conducted raids along the West African coast to secure their first captives. They also entered into alliances with African merchants and political elites to secure slaves for the trade. Through much of the 16th century, this was the dominant form of enslaved African labor procurement. It was also the only time that Europeans were significantly involved in the initial capture and enslavement of Africans in Africa.

Beginning in the 17th century and continuing through the abolition of the trade, African merchants and commercial and political elites controlled the continental slave trade. Over the course of its 400-year history, some 200 nation-states and thousands of leaders organized and managed the trading activities. Eventually 12 to 15 million Africans were sold to Europeans to work in the American colonial economies. As time went by, more and more of the captives were taken from farther and farther in the interior of West and Central Africa. European traders were obliged to purchase their captives from African merchants and rulers. Although many traditional African societies were disrupted by the expansion of the trade, and millions of Africans were

Opposite right and above:
BOUND MANDINGO, CIRCA 1900
WOOD SCULPTURE, NIGERIA
Captive men, women, and children were marched hundreds of miles from inland to coastal slave-trading posts. Often 5 to 10 percent of the captives died, or were killed in rebellion, during the long march to the sea—and to ships that would transport them to the Americas.

Opposite left:
BOUND AFRICAN WOMAN, CARVED
WOOD, GHANA
Artist unknown. Circa 1900.

victimized by its exigencies, many African rulers and commercial elites, like their European and colonial American counterparts, benefited immensely from the trade. So did such esteemed African states and kingdoms as Dahomey, Oyo, Congo, and Ashanti, to name a few.

Slavery had existed in Africa since ancient times. Like the civilizations of ancient Egypt, Greece, Rome, medieval Europe, and China, or the Incas and Aztecs of the Americas, many African societies were also slave societies. Slavery was still extremely widespread when the European traders arrived on the coast of West Africa. The capture, purchase, and sale of slaves were regular features of many African societies' commercial and social lives. Much of this commercial enterprise was for the domestic trade among diverse peoples and societies on the continent. In addition, flourishing Arab-controlled trans-Saharan and Indian Ocean slave trades had been supplying Africans slaves since the seventh century. An estimated seven million Africans were believed to have been enslaved and sold abroad in these two trades. They provided African laborers for Europe, the Mediterranean region, Arabia, and India. Slavery and the trade in slaves in Africa, then, were not European inventions.

The origins of slavery in African societies, like its origins throughout the world, can likely be traced to warfare on the continent and the problem that prisoners of war posed for the winners of military conflicts. As in other parts of the world, wars were initially waged for political reasons. These included the expansion of political boundaries; the defense of one's people, land, or resources; the destruction or nullification of a potential enemy; the acquisition of new wealth; or the defense of one's prerogatives. African rulers and societies went to war for all of these reasons. Given the political fragmentation that had characterized the African continent for much of its history prior to the development of the transatlantic slave trade, it is not surprising that internecine wars were waged continuously. Victors in these struggles were faced with one of five choices regarding their war prisoners. They could kill them, deport them, sell them, ransom them, or incorporate them into their societies. Women and children were frequently sold into the Arab slave trade. Some were retained as part of the slave labor force in the ruling society. Prior to the expansion of the transatlantic slave trade, men were killed, deported, ransomed, or sold. Selected men, however, were made slaves in their new societies as well and obliged to serve either in the victor's army or in other administrative posts. Inevitably, when the demand for slaves

Above:

**SLAVE TRADER AND SLAVE COFFLE,
CIRCA 1900, WOOD SCULPTURE,
WEST AFRICA**

*African artisan's depiction of mulatto slave
traders moving slaves in a coffle—a word
that comes from the Arabic* kafilah, *meaning
the chaining together of men, or animals,
for transport.*

Left:

**"SLAVERS REVENGING THEIR
LOSSES," WOOD ENGRAVING, 1866**

*An Arab slave driver murders an enslaved
African unable to keep up with the yoked
convoy marching from the African interior to a
coastal fort for delivery to traders.*

**CARVED IVORY TUSK,
CIRCA 1850, CONGO**

*Scenes of the slave trade carved on an elephant tusk
depict dramatic episodes, including the seizing of Africans
by slave traders, a forced march, sexual assault, and
exchanges between African and European slave traders.*

increased, the political motives for war were complemented and at times displaced by economic ones. States and societies sometimes went to war to secure slaves for sale in the burgeoning slave-trade markets. In addition, political and commercial elites acquired slaves as a means of expanding their personal wealth, power, and prestige. When the Europeans arrived in Africa seeking to purchase slaves for the transatlantic slave trade, there was a large class of people scattered throughout the continent who were legally slaves and available for purchase provided they had not been born in the household. There were also established methods of procurement and sale. The steady, unquenchable demand for slave labor triggered by the establishment and expansion of European colonial economies in the Americas tapped into this existing reservoir and made extraordinary demands of it. African political and economic elites at times became reluctant partners in this nefarious trade.

Between 1500 and the 1860s millions of Africans were captured, enslaved, and transported to the Americas. For the vast majority, especially after the 16th century, the enslavement process began in the interior of Africa's western coast. Prisoners who were casualties of wars became candidates for the trade. Some states transformed themselves into slave-trading nations and waged wars or carried out organized raids on villages to secure their captives. Renegades and bandit groups who recognized the economic potential of the trade carried out organized raids in the interior, capturing or kidnapping individuals or intercepting slave coffles en route to the coast and abducting the captives. Individuals who committed crimes such as murder, adultery, sorcery, or treason were sold into slavery as a form of punishment. In times of famine or other natural or man-made calamities, individuals sold or pawned themselves and/or their families to wealthier individuals in order to survive. The individuals who ended up crossing the Atlantic included Africans who had been enslaved through all of these methods. The overwhelming majority, however, were war prisoners and refugees.

Over the years, the internecine wars in Africa became more frequent, more deadly, and more efficient as a means of supplying African captives for the slave trade. The diffusion of European firearms changed the nature of warfare and raiding and increased the supply of African captives exponentially. An estimated 20 million guns were exported to West Africa between 1750 and 1807. These firearms became a major currency in the trade for slaves. People were literally traded for guns. And these firearms became the dominant weapons used in African warfare and slave raiding and provided security for caravans of slave captives between the interior and the coast.

Following capture and initial sale in the interior, transportation to the coast became the first of several life-threatening migrations for the African captives. This often brutal experience has been called the "Long March."

COWRIE SHELLS, TRADE CURRENCY
Though these cowrie shells are used as an Ibeji adornment, cowries were a popular currency in the slave trade. In the 16th century, 6,000 cowries purchased one slave, the price rising to 40,000 cowries by 1650. From 1700 to 1800 over 25 million pounds of cowries were exchanged in West Africa with European traders.

CURRENCY OF THE SLAVE TRADE

A variety of monetary currencies were used in the slave trade, including gold, silver, copper, iron, guns, gunpowder, livestock, tobacco, textiles, liquor, glass, and shells. Favored currencies included cowrie shells, which were desired by many African slave traders. During the 18th century, more than 25 million pounds of cowries, which were coveted culturally as charms for personal prosperity and fertility, were bartered between European and African slave traders. Cowrie values ranged from a few thousand to over 100,000 shells per slave. Other popular currencies included rifles and guns (at one to six per slave) and horses, with each generally valued at from one to twenty-five slaves per animal.

By the 1700s, rum had become the preferred currency in the slave trade, and distilleries were built in England and the American colonies specifically to supply slave ships with rum. From 1776 to 1807, Rhode Island exported more than 10 million gallons of

specially branded "Guinea rum" to Africa in exchange for slaves. By the American Revolution, rum was New England's major export, accounting for more than four-fifths of its total exports. The rum exchange for slaves ranged from about 130 gallons for one adult male to 110 gallons for one adult woman. Children sold for about 80 gallons of rum each.

At resale in the Americas, domestic slave auction prices usually reflected yearly labor costs for white workers. Prices for an adult male or female slave generally equaled the cost of one to two years' annual wage for a free worker.

Clockwise from bottom left:
KISSI, IRON *West African currency*
MANILLAS, CIRCA 1500 *Copper currency*
BEADS, CIRCA 1800, GLASS *Brazilian currency*
BEADS, CIRCA 1800, AGATE *Brazilian currency*
KATANGA CROSS, CIRCA 1500 *Copper currency, West Africa*

The trek from the interior to the coast could be as long as 300 miles. Slaves were shackled at the ankle, sometimes two abreast. They were then linked one (or two) behind the other in coffles (caravans) by either ropes or chains fitted around their necks. Sometimes forked tree branches substituted for ropes and chains. Armed guards and slave merchants/traders, sometimes mounted on horseback, shepherded these slave coffles to the coast. Merchant traders purchased or sold slaves along the way. The rigors of the forced march in tropical heat cost many their lives. Others arrived on the coast sick, dehydrated, or emaciated and had to be nursed back to physical and mental health before they could be offered for sale abroad. Those who managed to survive the Long March were imprisoned in slave castles, or holding pens, known as barracoons until they were sold and shipped to the Americas in the Middle Passage. The overwhelming majority of these captives had not seen a European prior to their arrival on the coast. Europeans controlled the transatlantic slave trade outside of Africa and on the coast. But on the continent, it was under the control of African political and economic elites and slave-trading states.

The Middle Passage

The Middle Passage experience began on the West African coast. It was along this shoreline that the captives who had been brought to the coast from the interior were transferred from African to European control. Each of the major European slave-trading powers established forts and trading posts along the Atlantic shore. Many were located on islands off the coast to improve security. For those who were sick or otherwise debilitated because of the rigors of the Long March, the barracoons and slave castles included medical treatment and at times psychological support. Healthy arrivals were kept healthy but under prisonlike conditions until the ships came. The wait could be months and sometimes years. Ships were also used as holding pens when they were in port.

The formal transfer of the captives from Africans to Europeans took place in marketlike settings. European traders inspected them and selected those they wished to add to their cargo. Some slave ships called and traded at several ports along the coast before they could purchase enough captives to make the Middle Passage voyage profitable. This could take from three to ten months. Guns, cowrie shells, glass beads, iron bars, manillas, rum, cloth, and

Opposite top:

"GROUP OF NEGROS, AS IMPORTED TO BE SOLD FOR SLAVES," SURINAM
Artist: William Blake

Opposite:

MUSKET WITH TALISMAN, CIRCA 1810
Wood and iron. The attached ivory amulet was believed to provide the weapon's African musketeer with magical powers, protecting him from death in war or battle, and from enslavement.

Below:

COFFLE CHAIN WITH SIX SHACKLES, CIRCA 1830, IRON
Shackles and heavy iron chains were used to transport a coffle, or gang of slaves. Specifically, coffles were trains or groups of men or beasts fastened or chained and driven along together.

other European commodities were traded for slaves. By the time the captives reached the coastal trading grounds, they might already have been sold two or more times to different African slaveholders. European traders were required to pay tribute, taxes, and other fees to political leaders in order to secure the right to trade as well as to receive the ruler's protection.

Initially, the ships that transported the Africans from Africa to the Americas were designed to carry a variety of trade goods as well as passengers. Gradually, as the trade evolved, more efficiently designed ships dedicated exclusively to the slave trade were manufactured in European and American shipyards. On average, they were midsize ships of 200 tons and carried an average of 350 slave passengers. By the end of the legal trade, some vessels were capable of carrying up to 1,000 people. Most ships after the 17th century had two decks, one of which was dedicated to carrying slave cargo. Men were chained together in pairs, laid flat or spoon-fashion, and shackled between decks with little space to stretch out or move around. Men were kept on one end of the deck behind a restraining wall. Women and children were kept on the opposite side of the wall, frequently unshackled. But they, like the men, had little space to move about between the decks. Women and children were allowed on deck frequently, but security concerns restricted males to the hold except at feeding and exercise time. Even then, the men were shackled and kept under heavy guard. The average height between decks ranged from three to five feet, and the average space allotted each person was sixteen inches by five and a half feet.

Food and water supplies for Middle Passages frequently proved inadequate. Provisions allotted for each trip were tightly budgeted for a specific number of captives and a specific length of voyage. The quality of the provisions, which consisted mainly of beans, rice, corn, yams, and small amounts of salted meat or fish, left much to be desired. Slave-ship captains were not above overstocking their vessels to increase their profits. This reduced the amount of food and water available for each passenger, which was usually insufficient. If the voyage lasted longer than planned, the food and water supplies were further taxed.

Mortality rates were high on the Middle Passage—estimates range from 15 to 20 percent of all the captives that disembarked from Africa. The voyage to the Americas could last from one to three months. Mortality rates tended

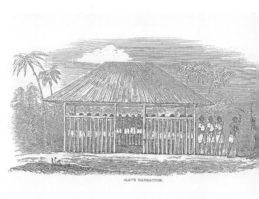

Above:
SLAVE BARRACOON, SIERRA LEONE, CIRCA 1840s
Chained by the neck and legs, recently captured Africans could be held under guard in a barracoon and flogged, sometimes fatally, if they resisted or tried to escape.

Opposite:
CAPE COAST CASTLE DUNGEON DOORS, WOOD, CAPE COAST, GHANA

H	Knots	½	Courses	Winds	
1	1	—	SW	SE	Monday Nov.r 30th 1750.
2	3	5½			This 24 hours Moderate
3	3	5½	SWbS	SbS	Breeze of Wind at 7 AM
4	3	5½			got up our sails to dry
5	3	—			
6			SW½W		
7	3	—	SWbS		
8	3	3	SW	SE	Dyed a Male slave
9	2	4			
10		5			
11	2	4	SWbW		Course — SW
12	2	6	SW	—	Dist — 72
13	2	5	SWbS	SbS	Diff.a Latt.de — 51
14	2	4	—		Dep. — 51
15	2	4	WSW	WbS	Latt by dead Rckg.ma — 8.47
16	2	5	SW½S		Obs.on — 8.47
17		5			Diff Long.a — 55
18		4	WSW		
19		2			
20	2	5			

to increase with the length of the voyage. They declined over the course of the trade from 25 percent in the early 18th century to 5 to 10 percent in the mid-19th century because trips were shorter and more health precautions were taken. However, between 1850 and 1867, the percentage of deaths increased in part because of "over packing."

Dehydration was the major cause of death among the captives. Seasickness caused vomiting, dysentery was spread by bad food and water, and diarrhea increased the incidence of dehydration among the passengers. So did the threat of exhaustion brought on by the stifling temperatures between the decks. Epidemic diseases—smallpox, yellow fever, typhoid fever, and measles, among others—killed many slaves and crew members, sometimes entire shiploads. Despondent enslaved Africans also committed or attempted to commit suicide to escape their plight. The mortality rates notwithstanding, upward of 75 percent of the captives waged successful struggles against their oppression and dehumanization, survived the torturous voyage, and planted the human seeds in the Americas from which the African populations in the United States and the rest of the Americas evolved. An estimated 36,000 voyages were needed to transport the estimated 10 million Africans who survived the Middle Passage and settled in the Americas.

Security was a paramount concern of slave ship captains and their crews. The security threat loomed on the African coast, where records show that more than 60 ships were attacked by Africans trying to rescue slave captives. Resistance activities and revolts of slave passengers were not uncommon. Crewmen on slave ships were a mixed breed—both seamen and prison guards. They were heavily armed throughout the voyage. So were the ships, whose cannon and other armaments were rigged out as much to police the captives as to defend the ship against external attacks. In times of resistance

Above:
SLAVE BRANDING IRON, CIRCA 1790
Branding was common throughout the slavery era. The general practice of many slave traffickers was to brand slaves twice, once upon purchase in Africa and a second time at sale in the Americas.

Opposite (overlay):
LOG OF SLAVE SHIP "LAWRANCE," 1730-1731
Commander Abraham Dumaresq's daily and hourly record of the transatlantic journey of the British slave ship Lawrance *from Angola to Argentina details the deaths of 65 slaves. From November 16, 1730, to January 14, 1731, 33 men, 31 women, and 1 boy, as Commander Dumaresq reports, "dyed" (died) during the voyage. Probably 600 or more slaves were aboard the* Lawrance *at the start of its journey.*

Opposite:
THE AFRICANS OF THE SLAVE BARK "WILDFIRE," JUNE 2, 1860, HARPER'S WEEKLY
Slave-trader efforts to keep their human cargo in the crowded hull below "healthy" usually meant bringing slaves on deck two or three times weekly for fresh air and exercise. While on deck, crew members or slave workers went below to scrub and clean the heavily soiled decks. Planking was scraped and swabbed of human waste. Often red-hot iron pellets were dropped into pots of vinegar to freshen the foul air in the galleys below. On deck or below, slaves remained shackled. Segregated by sex, slaves were kept apart from others of their own nationality, language, and tribe.

ENSLAVED AFRICANS ABOARD A SLAVE SHIP

Deaths were a daily occurrence during the sea voyage from Africa to the Americas, with sickness, disease, rebellion, and suicide taking many lives. A common cause of death was the depletion of freshwater supplies during long voyages, which caused many slaves to perish when they were given salt water to drink. Surviving ship logs indicate that onboard fatalities were generally 15 to 20 percent of the transported slave population. An estimated three million to five million enslaved men, women, and children perished during the Middle Passage experience.

or revolt, crewmen were enlisted into the slave-ship captain's army to put down the uprising. Africans who have left us records of their perspective on the Middle Passage experience report that at the outset, they had no idea of where they were going or why. Many were concerned that they were going to be eaten by the white men. They complained that they were not adequately fed; were physically and sexually abused by crewmen; and had to sleep in urine-, vomit-, and feces-laden decks and breathe putrid air. They also reported that they were relieved to learn, upon arrival in the Americas, that they were only being told to work.

On board slave ships, in the midst of their oppression, the African captives, who were often as much strangers to themselves as to their European captors, forged the first links in their new American identities. Relationships established during the Middle Passage based on their shared oppression frequently resulted in revolts and other forms of resistance that bound them in new social and political alliances. Far from wiping out all traces of their African past, the Middle Passage experience introduced them to other Africans and provided opportunities for them to begin to draw on their collective African heritages to make themselves a new people. Today the 10 million original survivors have produced progeny that number between 150 and 200 million people of African descent throughout the hemisphere. They are the first and most fundamental evidence of blacks' triumph over slavery.

Above:

BARTERING FOR SLAVES ON THE GOLD COAST, CIRCA 1850

Figure in left foreground holds a three-person ship shackle. Outside shackles held two adults or adolescents seated in one direction. Middle shackles held the person seated opposite.

Opposite:

"MARIE SÉRAPHIQUE" OF NANTES, 1773

French slave ship shown moored off Cap Français, Saint Domingue, Hispaniola. On board, white gentlemen and ladies enjoy a picnic while others examine the human cargo.

Below:

MIDDLE PASSAGE IRONS, CIRCA 1700

Adults as well as children were frequently immobilized with irons such as these during the transatlantic crossing to North America, South America, and the Caribbean.

ELMINA CASTLE, GHANA
Fisherman Kweku Tikgay navigates past the imposing fortress built in 1482 by Portuguese traders. The Dutch captured Elmina in 1637, a victory that symbolized their forceful entry into the African slave trade.

No.		Age.	Capacity.
1	Aleck,	33	Carpenter.
2	Mary Ann,	31	Field hand, prime.
3—3	Louisa,	10	
4	Abram,	25	Prime field hand.
5	Judy,	24	Prime field hand.
6	Carolina,	5	
	Simon,	1½	
—8	Daphne, infant.		
	Daniel,	45	Field hand, not prime.
16	Philis,	32	Field hand.
11			
13	Margaret,	4	
1+		2	
—15	Hannah,	2 months.	

CHAPTER 2

THE PRICE OF CHAINS

African peoples were captured and transported to the Americas to work. Most European colonial economies in the Americas from the 16th through the 19th century were dependent on enslaved African labor for their survival. According to European colonial officials, the abundant land they had "discovered" in the Americas was useless without sufficient labor to exploit it. Slavery systems of labor exploitation were preferred, but neither European nor Native American sources proved adequate to the task. The trans-Saharan slave trade had long supplied enslaved African labor to work on sugar plantations in the Mediterranean alongside white slaves from Russia and the Balkans. This same trade also sent as many as 10,000 slaves a year to serve owners in North Africa, the Middle East, and the Iberian Peninsula.

Having proved themselves competent workers in Europe and on nascent sugar plantations on the Madeira and Canary Islands off the coast of Africa, enslaved Africans became the labor force of choice in the Western Hemisphere—so much so that they became the overwhelming majority of the colonial populations of the Americas. Of the 6.5 million immigrants who survived the crossing of the Atlantic and settled in the Western Hemisphere between 1492 and 1776, only 1 million were Europeans. The remaining 5.5 million were African. An average of 80 percent of these enslaved Africans—men, women, and children—were employed, mostly as field-workers. Women as well as children worked in some capacity. Only very young children (under six), the elderly, the sick, and the infirm escaped the day-to-day work routine.

Opposite:

RETURNING FROM THE COTTON FIELD IN SOUTH CAROLINA, CIRCA 1870

Workers bring cotton in as dusk approaches. Slave labor was generally divided into two types of work systems, gang and task. Gangs worked under the supervision of (slave) drivers and overseers, often working six days a week. Slaves who worked under the task system were assigned a specific amount of work to complete in a day or week and were then generally free to use their time as they chose once their assignments were completed. The task system enabled many enslaved laborers, artisans, craftsmen, craftswomen, and entrepreneurs to accumulate money and property by allowing them to work for themselves during their "free time."

Opposite (overlay) and below:

BROADSIDE ANNOUNCING SALE OF 25 SLAVES, 1852, CHARLESTON, SOUTH CAROLINA

GANG OF 25 SEA ISLAND COTTON AND RICE NEGROES,

By LOUIS D. DE SAUSSURE.

On *THURSDAY* the 25th Sept., 1852, at 11 o'clock, A.M., will be sold at RYAN'S MART, in Chalmers Street, in the City of Charleston,

A prime gang of 25 Negroes, accustomed to the culture of Sea Island Cotton and Rice.

More than half of the enslaved African captives in the Americas were employed on sugar plantations. Sugar developed into the leading slave-produced commodity in the Americas. During the 16th and 17th centuries, Brazil dominated the production of sugarcane. One of the earliest large-scale manufacturing industries was established to convert the juice from the sugarcane into sugar, molasses, and eventually rum, the alcoholic beverage of choice of the triangular trade. Ironically, the profits made from the sale of these goods in Europe, as well as the trade in these commodities in Africa, were used to purchase more slaves.

During the 18th century, Saint Domingue (Haiti) surpassed Brazil as the leading sugar-producing colony. The number of slaves brought to the tiny island of Haiti equaled more than twice the number imported into the United States. The vast majority came during the 18th century to work in the expanding sugar plantation economy. The Haitian Revolution abolished slavery there and led to the establishment of the first black republic in the Americas. It also ended Haiti's dominance of world sugar production.

Cuba assumed this position during the 19th century, and even after slavery was abolished there in 1886, sugar remained the foundation of its economy and its primary export commodity throughout the 20th century. Sugar was also produced by slave labor in the other Caribbean islands as well as in Louisiana in the United States.

During the colonial period in the United States, tobacco was the dominant slave-produced commodity. Concentrated in Virginia and Maryland, tobacco plantations utilized the largest percentage of enslaved Africans imported into the United States prior to the American Revolution. Rice and indigo plantations in South Carolina also employed enslaved African labor. The American Revolution cost Virginia and Maryland their principal European tobacco markets, and for a brief period of time after the Revolution, the future of slavery in the United States was in jeopardy. Most of the northern states abolished it, and even Virginia debated abolition in the Virginia Assembly.

The invention of the cotton gin in 1793 gave slavery a new life in the United States. Between 1800 and 1860, slave-produced cotton expanded from South Carolina and Georgia to newly colonized lands west of the Mississippi. This shift of the slave economy from the upper South (Virginia and Maryland) to the lower South was accompanied by a comparable shift

Men, women, and children were sold at auction or at town or city markets where chattel, goods, and commodities were traded daily. Agents placed advertisements in newspapers and on posters in taverns, shops, and public announcement boards. Sales took place on ship decks or at auction blocks on piers, in slave pens, or in stores.

Commonly, captives who survived the Atlantic crossing were "freshened"—cleaned, shaved, and made presentable for sale. For a healthy appearance, oils were applied to their skin, salves and lotions were used to hide scars from beatings and diseases, and older slaves were made to look younger by blackening their gray hairs. Trial periods and short-term guarantees of a slave's good health were the norm. Buyers lost nothing if, during a one-week period, a slave died, became ill, or ran away. For auctions or sales, slave registries were prepared and slaves were sold according to age, sex, and occupation. Planters either negotiated the price of a preset number of slaves or bid for slaves by auction or "scramble." In the scramble, planters or their representatives marked individuals or groups of slaves with collars, handkerchiefs, or ropes. Skilled and semi-skilled workers, i.e., those with metal- and wood-working talent, or from African regions where rice, cotton, and sugar were cultivated, were "tagged" for easy identification of their work experience.

New York City was the northern hub of slave-trading activity. In 1711 a slave market opened on an East River pier at Wall Street, where slave auctions and sales were held weekly. Enslaved native Americans and indentured servants were also sold at market, including periodic shiploads of African children under the age of 13. Though New York City had a slave population of about 15 percent during the colonial era, most slaves shipped to New York were redirected to southern and Caribbean ports.

PLANTATION SLAVE QUARTERS, CIRCA MID-1800S, ST. HELENA ISLAND, SOUTH CAROLINA

of the enslaved African population to the lower South and West. After the abolition of the slave trade in 1808, the principal source of the expansion of slavery into the lower South was the domestic slave trade from the upper South. By 1850, 1.8 million of the 2.5 million enslaved Africans employed in agriculture in the United States were working on cotton plantations.

The vast majority of enslaved Africans employed in plantation agriculture were field hands. Even on plantations, however, they worked in other capacities. Some were domestics and worked as butlers, waiters, maids, seamstresses, and launderers. Others were assigned as carriage drivers, hostlers, and stable boys. Artisans—carpenters, stonemasons, blacksmiths, millers, coopers, spinners, and weavers—were also employed as part of plantation labor forces.

Enslaved Africans also worked in urban areas. Upward of 10 percent of the enslaved African population in the United States lived in cities. Charleston, Richmond, Savannah, Mobile, New York, Philadelphia, and New Orleans all had sizable slave populations. In the southern cities they totaled approximately a third of the population. The range of slave occupations in cities was vast. Domestic servants dominated, but there were carpenters, fishermen, coopers, draymen, sailors, masons, bricklayers, blacksmiths, bakers, tailors, peddlers, painters, and porters. Although most worked directly for their owners, others were hired out to work as skilled laborers on plantations, on public works projects, and in industrial enterprises. A small percentage hired themselves out and paid their owners a percentage of their earnings.

Each plantation economy was part of a larger national and international political economy. The cotton plantation economy, for instance, is generally seen as part of the regional economy of the American South. By the 1830s, "cotton was king" indeed in the South. It was also king in the United States, which was competing for economic leadership in the global political economy. Plantation-grown cotton was the foundation of the antebellum southern economy. But the American financial and shipping industries were also dependent on slave-produced cotton. So was the British textile industry. Cotton was not shipped directly to Europe from the South. Rather, it was shipped to New York and then transshipped to England and other centers of cotton manufacturing in the United States and Europe. As the cotton plantation economy expanded throughout the southern region, banks and financial houses in New York supplied the loan capital and/or investment capital to purchase land and slaves.

Recruited as an inexpensive source of labor, enslaved Africans in the United States also became important economic and political capital in the American political economy. Enslaved Africans were legally a form of property—a commodity. Individually and collectively, they were frequently used as collateral in all kinds of business transactions. They were also traded for other kinds of goods and services. The value of the investments slaveholders held in their slaves was often used to secure loans to purchase additional land or slaves. Slaves were also used to pay off outstanding debts. When calculating the value of estates, the estimated value of each slave was included. This became the source of tax revenue for local and state governments. Taxes were also levied on slave transactions.

Politically, the U.S. Constitution incorporated a feature that made enslaved Africans political capital—to the benefit of southern states. The so-called three-fifths compromise allowed the southern states to count their slaves as three-fifths of a person for purposes of calculating states' representation in the U.S. Congress. Thus the balance of power between slaveholding and non-slaveholding states turned, in part, on the three-fifths presence of enslaved Africans in the census. Slaveholders were taxed on the same three-fifths principle, and no taxes paid on slaves supported the national treasury. In sum, the slavery system in the United States was a national system that touched the very core of its economic and political life.

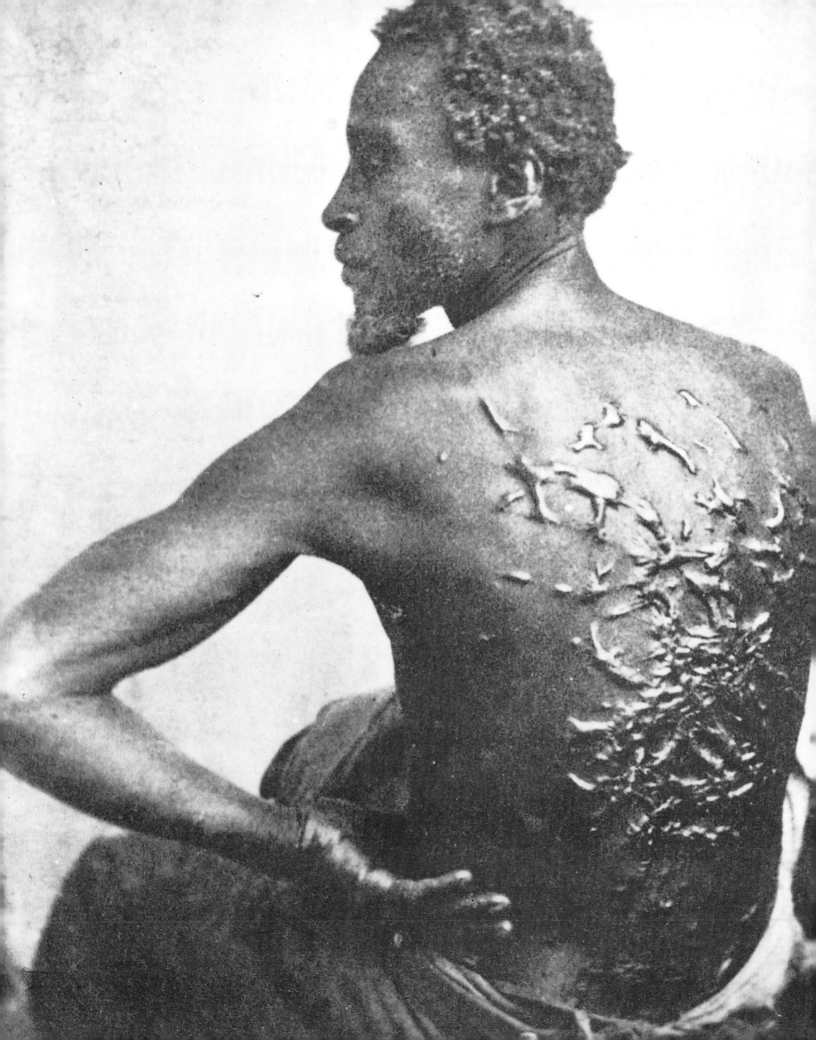

The Call to Work

SLAVE WORK HORN, (above) circa 1860. Crafted from wood and cow horn, this slave work horn was used on a South Carolina plantation to call slaves to and from work. After the Civil War, the horn was used to call newly freed black children to school.

At the sound of a work horn, slaves toiled from "can see to can't," a saying that described the span of their daily labor from sunrise to well past sundown. Depending on the region, the economy of the New World (the Americas) depended on slave labor for the production of many crops and commodities, including sugar, tobacco, coffee, cotton, rice, and rum.

The first widespread use of slave labor in the colonial United States was for **TOBACCO** production. From the arrival of the first Africans (indentured servants) in Virginia in 1619, black and white indentures worked in the colony's early tobacco fields. But without enough indentured or free workers to meet the export demand for production of high-quality Virginia tobacco, slave laborers were brought into the colony. Tobacco planters found that slave labor produced the greatest tobacco profits. In Virginia, the black population increased from about 5 percent of the population in 1660 to more than 40 percent by 1760.

But the invention of the cotton gin in 1793 contributed most greatly to the slave population in the United States. In two years, U.S. exports of **COTTON** jumped from 138,000 pounds to more than 1,600,000 pounds. Between 1790 and 1860 about a million slaves (twice the number of Africans shipped to the United States during the transatlantic slave trade) were transported or sold to cotton-producing and slave-holding territories.

The growing world demand for cotton caused slavery to spread into the new states of the Southwest. Alabama, Mississippi, and Louisiana became the heartland of "King Cotton"—America's cotton kingdom. By the Civil War, cotton was the South's chief crop and totaled 57 percent of all U.S. exports.

Cotton Basket, 1850. Wood. South Carolina.

Cotton porter, Savannah, Georgia, circa 1885

Principally because of its reliance on agriculture, the South resisted the industrialization that transformed the North in the 19th century. Therefore the South manufactured little, and most manufactured goods had to be imported from Europe or purchased from the North.

Though cotton production was an important factor in the U.S. slave population, throughout the hemisphere, the majority of the 10 million enslaved Africans worked on **SUGAR** plantations, with more than half the number of slaves producing sugarcane and its by-products—sugar, rum, and molasses.

Following pages:
CANE CUTTERS IN JAMAICA, CIRCA 1880
In 1655 England took control of Jamaica from Spain and transformed the island from a modest cocoa-producing region to an enormously profitable plantation economy of slave-produced sugar, rum, and molasses. Jamaica served as a major British port in the transatlantic slave trade, providing rest and supplies for vessels en route to South Carolina, Massachusetts, and New York. Of the estimated 10 million African slaves transported to the Americas, nearly 2 million were transported through Jamaican ports.

Field hands bring in the "whole week's picking."
Collage art by William Henry Brown from a visit to Nitta Yuma,
a cotton plantation in Vicksburg, Mississippi, 1842.

*Slave laborers cutting lumber into boards,
Brazil, circa 1835*

Wheelwrights at work, circa 1860

SKILLED LABORERS

"...So many negroes are trained up to be handicraft tradesmen, to the discouragement of Your Majesty's white subjects..." wrote a colonial adviser to King George II in 1733, foreseeing that in the Carolinas and elsewhere, skilled black craftsmen (free and enslaved) were limiting job opportunities for white immigrants. With more Europeans arriving, laws were written to stop black artisans from becoming a liability to white employment.

In some colonies blacks outnumbered whites in the carpentry, wheelwright, cooper (barrel-making), and smithing crafts. In New York white coopers petitioned the colonial legislature to prohibit blacks from the craft, claiming the need for protection against "the pernicious custom of breeding slaves to trades whereby honest and industrious tradesmen are reduced to poverty for want of employ." In Charleston, New Orleans, and Richmond, black artisans dominated the blacksmithing craft. In 1756 a South Carolina law imposed a fine of five pounds a day for allowing a slave to work alone. The law required one white to be hired for every two slaves.

In 1800 a "slave badge" system was introduced in Charleston to regulate the number of slave hires—for owners who wanted to rent out their slaves, or for slaves with time available to hire out themselves. Enacted to encourage the hiring of white workers, the badge system taxed slave labor, employing what is considered an early form of "affirmative action" by some historians. All southern states (and some northern states) regulated the hiring of skilled and semi-skilled slaves and free blacks by laws that benefited white male immigrants, who were often trained by black craftsmen.

Above: **SLAVE HIRE BADGES, CIRCA EARLY 1800S. SOUTH CAROLINA**
Above, right: **QUARTERMASTER'S WHARF, ALEXANDRIA, VIRGINIA, 1863**
Below: **SLAVE PASS, JUNE 1, 1843**

Please to let Benjamin McDaniel pass to Dr. Henkel's in New-Market Shenandoah County, Va. and return on Monday or Tuesday next to Montpellier, for Mrs. Madison

June 1st 1843.

A Rebel Negro armed & on his guard.

ROUTES TO FREEDOM

The central theme of black history in the United States and throughout the Western Hemisphere has been the struggle for freedom. From the period of captivity on the continent, through the Middle Passage, and to the period of enslavement in the Americas, the freedom quest was the central motivating factor in black social, political, economic, and cultural behavior. Though most enslaved Africans were legally enslaved for life, as were their children, they used a variety of ways to liberate themselves and their families from slavery. Some ran away to the city, to the North, to the swamps, or to the mountains. Others organized or participated in rebellions. Some carried out acts of day-to-day resistance. Some volunteered for military service in exchange for the promise of freedom. Still others worked and earned sufficient money to buy their freedom.

Toward the end of the 18th century, the moral, ethical, and ideological foundations of the slave trade and slavery began to crumble. Manumission and abolition societies sprang up, slave rebellions and revolts developed, and newly formed states and societies passed laws abolishing slavery. Enslaved Africans took advantage of these opportunities and used them to liberate themselves and their loved ones. The Civil War and the 13th Amendment to the Constitution ended slavery in the United States, and by 1890 slavery had been abolished throughout the hemisphere.

Runaways, Rebels, and Maroons

Among the largest group of enslaved Africans who triumphed over slavery were those who stole themselves—those who ran away, taking with them the value that their "owners" had paid for them, the value of the labor their "masters" hoped to extract from them, and the value of their knowledge and skills. Wherever slavery existed, enslaved Africans ran away. Some ran away for short periods of time to protest treatment or to force masters and overseers to renegotiate their relationships with their enslaved captives. Others ran away to reunite themselves with family members who had been sold away, or

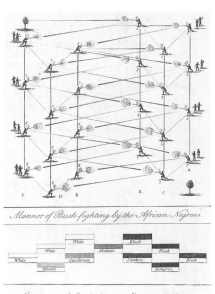

Manner of Bush-fighting by the African Negroes.

Gradation of Shades between Europe & Africa.

Above:

DIAGRAM OF MAROON GUERRILLA WARFARE TACTICS

This account of a Dutch military expedition to suppress a rebellion of Surinam maroons includes an account of their guerrilla warfare tactics.

Opposite:

A REBEL NEGRO ARMED AND ON HIS GUARD, 1796

Illustration from Narrative of a Five Years' Expedition against the Revolted Negroes of Surinam *by Captain John G. Stedman.*

PROCEEDINGS

OF THE

Governor and Affembly of Jamaica,

IN REGARD TO THE

MAROON NEGROES:

PUBLISHED BY ORDER OF THE ASSEMBLY.

TO WHICH IS PREFIXED,

AN INTRODUCTORY ACCOUNT,

CONTAINING,

OBSERVATIONS ON THE DISPOSITION, CHARACTER, MANNERS, AND HABITS OF LIFE,

OF THE MAROONS,

AND

A Detail of the Origin, Progrefs, and Termination

OF

THE LATE WAR BETWEEN THOSE PEOPLE AND THE WHITE INHABITANTS.

———

LONDON:

Printed for JOHN STOCKDALE, Piccadilly.

M.DCC.XCVI.

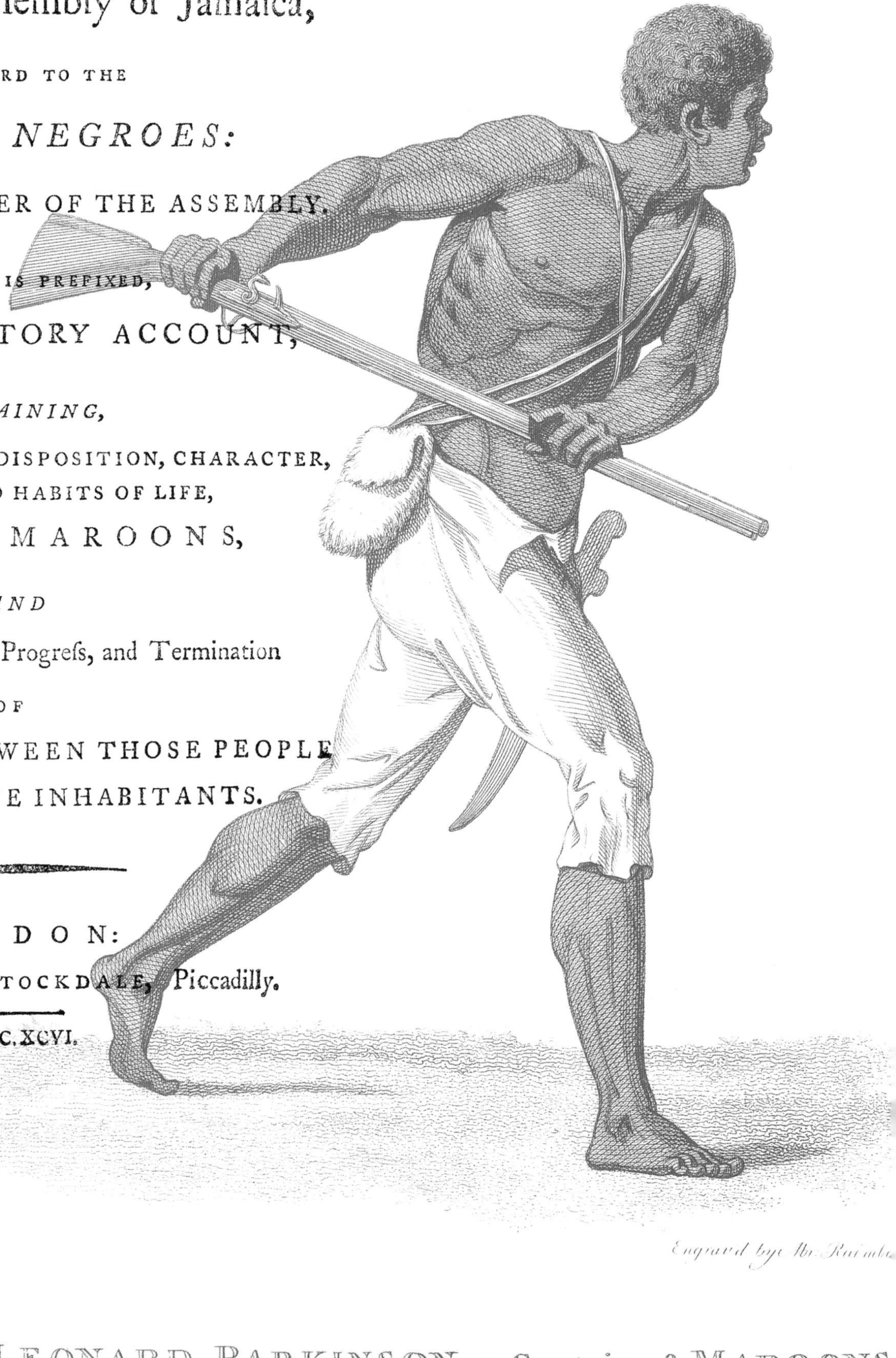

LEONARD PARKINSON, a Captain of MAROONS

to sustain familial or romantic liaisons. Some fled to seek personal freedom or to improve their economic lot. Some found refuge in urban areas, where they could hide in free black communities. Others took up refuge in Native American communities and free black towns. Still others ran away and created new "maroon" communities, where they set up their own systems of government and social organization and ran their own lives.

Upward of 50,000 enslaved Africans ran away each year in the American South prior to the Civil War. Most returned, took their punishment, and/or renegotiated their relationship with the institution of slavery. But their act of running away exposed the fundamental instability of slavery regimes and the degree to which these regimes were dependent on enslaved Africans, rather than the reverse. A significant minority of runaways disappeared into the ranks of free black communities in the South, the North, and abroad—from the Caribbean and Europe to Canada and Africa. Those who made it to the North became stalwart soldiers in the armies of abolitionists and anti-slavery workers there. Many, such as Frederick Douglass and Harriet Tubman, became leaders of the effort to abolish slavery in the United States. Others settled in Native American communities and became actively involved in their struggles against intruding colonial regimes. During the 1820s and 1830s, fugitive slaves played active and at times leadership roles in the two Seminole Wars.

Maroon communities and societies—organized enclaves of runaways—developed in the earliest stages of New World African slavery and continued through its abolition. Vibrant, highly organized maroon communities developed in Jamaica, Surinam, Brazil, Colombia, and North Carolina. Descendants of these maroons still live active lives rooted in their maroon heritage in Jamaica and Surinam.

Opposite:
LEONARD PARKINSON, A CAPTAIN OF MAROONS
From Jamaica Assembly, Proceedings in Regard to the Maroon Negroes. Jamaica, Seat of the Maroon War in 1795 and 1796. Drawn by J. Robertson. From The History of the Maroons *by R.C. Dallas, 1803.*
The maroons of Jamaica took to the hills and waged two wars against the British in the late 18th and early 19th centuries. Maroon communities of today's Jamaica continue to function as semi-autonomous communities.

Below:
DEATH OF CAPTAIN FERRER, THE CAPTAIN OF THE "AMISTAD," JULY 1839
Lithograph in A History of the Amistad Captives, *1840.*
Captured Africans frequently revolted on slave ships. Although shackles, chains, and guns were used to constrain them, they sometimes succeeded in overpowering their captors.

CHAINED AND SHACKLED

The slavery era produced an assortment of fetters, chains, shackles, manacles, and other human restraints. In the early African slave trade, captives were transported in caravans or coffles, their legs tied with rope and their necks encircled by wooden braces. But with escapes, resistance, and rebellions came stronger and more punitive apparatus.

Wrist, neck, or leg irons were fastened with a latch or padlock, or riveted permanently. Like the ball and chain, spiked ankle shackles and spiked collars were equipped to thwart and injure fugitives. Collars could discourage a runaway from ducking, lifting, climbing, or even sleeping. Ankle spikes were fashioned to deter walking or running. Manufactured in Europe, Africa, and the Americas, "slave irons" were made in sizes for adults and children.

Some restraints were medieval in origin, but many were designed specifically to curtail slave runaways, becoming staples for prisons, jails, and general law enforcement.

CRAB-STYLE RUNAWAY SHACKLES, CIRCA 1800, IRON
Noisy rattling beads in these shackles (styled like African ceremonial dance anklets) helped slave-catchers apprehend fugitives. Clever runaways inserted mudpies to muffle the sound.

SPIKED NECK COLLAR, CIRCA 1840, IRON
Designed to prevent any neck or shoulder movement

SPIKED ANKLE SHACKLE WITH BALL AND CHAIN, CIRCA 1860, IRON
Designed to thwart running away, the three-inch spikes could cause severe lacerations.

Nat Turner

THE FIGHT FOR FREEDOM

$200 Reward.

Ranaway from the subscriber, last night, a mulatto man named **FRANK MULLEN,** about twenty-one years old, five feet ten or eleven inches high. He wears his hair long at the sides and top, close behind, and keeps it nicely combed; rather thick lips, mild countenance, polite when spoken to, and very genteel in his person. His clothing consists of a variety of summer and winter articles, among which are a blue cloth coat and blue casinet coatee, white pantaloons, blue cloth do., and a pair of new ribbed casinet do., a blue Boston wrapper, with velvet collar, several black hats, boots, shoes, &c. As he has absconded without any provocation, it is presumed he will make for Pennsylvania or New-York. I will give one hundred dollars if taken in the State of Maryland, or the above reward if taken any where east of that State, and secured so that I get him again, and all reasonable expenses paid if brought home to the subscriber, living in the city of Washington.

THOS. C. SCOTT.

October 21, 1835.

Slave revolts and uprisings occurred throughout the slavery era—despite harsh and deadly reprisals. Colonial laws prohibited slave gatherings, restricted slave "privileges" and punished slaves severely for any activity that could lead to insurrection, including learning to read and write. More than 500 documented cases of rebellions on land and sea indicate that the potential for slave violence was monitored closely.

In 1526 the first enslaved Africans in continental North America arrived in South Carolina to provide labor for Spanish colonizers. They rebelled and fled into the wilderness frontier a few months later. In New York a group of enslaved Africans in 1712 set

Broadside Offering Reward for Runaway Slave Frank Mullen,
October 21, 1835, Washington, D.C.

Harriet Tubman

Frederick Douglass

Negro Abraham

fire to a building on Manhattan Island, on the outskirts of the city. The slaves ambushed whites who had come to put out the blaze, killing 8. In response, 13 blacks were hanged, one was chained and starved to death, one was burned at the stake, and another was "broken on the wheel." (The slave was strapped to the wheel and his limbs were broken with a hammer.)

The largest slave rebellion prior to the American Revolution took place on Sunday, September 9, 1739, near Charleston, South Carolina. Led by a male slave named Jemmy, 20 slaves went into a store, took guns, and beheaded the shopkeepers. Beating drums and shouting "liberty," the slaves marched along the Stono River, setting fire to plantations, killing slave owners, and freeing fellow slaves. Twenty-four whites were killed and at least 44 blacks executed; their severed heads were posted on fences. Stricter prohibitions against blacks were passed, including making it a crime to teach a slave to write, and the drum was banned.

The ideals of freedom, justice, and liberty were given new meaning by the American Revolution—and the bloody Haitian revolution, which had alarmed southern planters. In 1800 Gabriel Prosser (circa 1775-1800), a slave blacksmith, made plans for a slave insurrection to create an independent black state in Virginia. His plan included attacking an arsenal and powder house in Richmond, and killing all whites except Methodists, Quakers, and Frenchmen. Some historians believe that Gabriel's army of 1,000 slaves (estimates range up to 50,000 supporters) might have succeeded had it not been for a fierce rainstorm that flooded roads and washed out bridges. Governor James Monroe was informed of the plot and sent troops to stop the revolt. Gabriel and 26 of his followers were arrested, convicted, and hanged.

In 1822 Denmark Vesey (circa 1767-1822), a free carpenter who had purchased his own freedom in 1800 with $600 he had won in a street lottery, organized an uprising of Charleston slaves. His plan reportedly called for the burning of the city and the freeing of all slaves. Vesey and 34 companions were hanged and 31 supporters were exiled to slavery outside the colony.

Born a slave in Virginia, Nat Turner (1800-1831) led the most famous slave revolt in U.S. history in 1831. Seeing a vision of "white spirits and black spirits engaged in battle," Turner, a minister, organized and led a group of 60 black men on a rebellion in Southampton County, Virginia. Fifty-seven whites were killed, and in retaliation, over 100 blacks were killed, with more than a dozen severed heads set atop poles as public warnings. On October 30 Turner was captured in the Great Dismal Swamp (along the Virginia and North Carolina border) and publicly executed 12 days later. Turner's action set off a new wave of oppressive legislation prohibiting the education, movement, and assembly of slaves, and stiffened pro-slavery, anti-abolitionist convictions that persisted in the South until the Civil War.

Harriet Tubman and Frederick Douglass were two of the most famous runaways. **NEGRO ABRAHAM** (circa 1790-1870) fled to the Florida territory, becoming a leader among the native Seminole.

WATER PASSAGE

Many slaves traveled on foot during dark hours. Some used a drinking gourd as a nightly astronomical guide, aligning its shape to the Big Dipper constellation and journeying northward. To get away, some stole horses, stole away on ships, or piloted small crafts to cross lakes and rivers to make their way north along the Atlantic shore.

Military Service as a Route to Freedom

The process of colonizing the Americas turned them into a perpetual war zone. In addition to the military expeditions carried out against the Native American peoples, competing European colonial powers were constantly at war with each other, vying for the spoils of "discovery" and colonization—land, gold, silver, and other resources of the Native American populations. Under ideal circumstances, they would never have considered arming slaves. And throughout the colonial period, local and metropolitan legislatures passed laws forbidding blacks to carry firearms. But the Americas were anything but normal, and throughout the period of slavery, European colonizers were obliged to turn to Africans—free and enslaved—to help defend themselves against their respective enemies. This perpetual military situation offered some enslaved Africans opportunities to pursue their freedom quests through military service.

Enslaved Africans, who had built most of the forts and battle works, were frequently enlisted to serve in the defense forces of the colonial powers. They volunteered for service whenever the offer of freedom was one of the rewards. They fought, for instance, on the side of the British and the American colonists during the American Revolution because both sides offered freedom to those who served. They fought on both sides of the Civil War for the same reason.

Some armed themselves and fought for their own freedom. Maroon communities throughout the Americas waged guerrilla warfare campaigns and at times full-scale wars against European colonists. In the United States, rebels such as Gabriel Prosser, Nat Turner, and Denmark Vesey plotted, or took up arms, to overthrow slavery regimes. Haitian rebels Toussaint L'Ouverture, Dessalines, and Christophe succeeded, creating the first black republic in the hemisphere after defeating the military forces of Napoleonic France, England, and Spain, which were sent to put down the first successful slave rebellion in the Americas. The specter of the Haitian revolution loomed over every slave regime in the Americas until slavery was abolished, and the Haitian revolution inspired blacks in other slave societies to take up arms and fight for their freedom.

Opposite:

SEMINOLE INDIAN SOLDIER, CIRCA 1890

In the 18th century, a Florida community of fugitive slaves and native Americans were known as "seminoles," after the Creek word for "runaway." In the 1830s the U.S. military declared war on the Seminole but abandoned the effort after more than 1,500 U.S. soldiers were killed. Ironically, a few decades later the U.S. government enlisted the Seminole to battle the Plains Indians. Known as the Seminole Negro Indian Scouts, the unit became one of the most decorated of the western Indian war era. However, many of the Seminole soldiers were denied U.S. Army pensions.

Above:

THE BLACK PHALANX; A HISTORY OF THE NEGRO SOLDIER OF THE UNITED STATES IN THE WARS OF 1775-1812, 1861-65 BY JOSEPH T. WILSON

On the night of March 5, 1770, **CRISPUS ATTUCKS** (circa 1723-1770), a free black dockworker, marched with 50 laborers and sailors into a dangerous confrontation with British soldiers, whose presence in Boston was sharply resented. The soldiers fired into the crowd and Attucks fell instantly, becoming the first of five men to die in the Boston Massacre. American patriots hailed Attucks's heroism and declared it as the event that sparked the American Revolution.

Liberty, the buzzword of the American Revolution, caused heated discussions about slavery. In 1775 American Revolutionist Thomas Paine wrote an article for a Pennsylvania newspaper entitled "African Slavery in America," questioning the legality and morality of slavery. Only weeks later, the Philadelphia Quakers organized the first American anti-slavery society. By 1776 one-fifth of the colonial population were of African ancestry, of which about 95 percent were enslaved. During the next seven years blacks, free and enslaved, played an important role on both sides of the conflict.

Crispus Attucks, Boston Massacre, March 5, 1770

Unidentified Civil War (Union) Soldier, circa 1864

A Black Revolutionary War Soldier

Toussaint L'Ouverture and the Haitian Revolution

In November 1775 Lord Dunmore, the royal governor of Virginia, issued a proclamation that any slaves who fled to British lines and assisted in defeating the rebellion would be granted their freedom. In New York a British decree promised "every Negro who shall desert the Rebell Standdard full security to follow within these lines…."

As English forces traveled through the colonies, several thousand slaves joined the British side. They worked in labor battalions and took up arms against their former owners by enlisting in British army units, including the Black Pioneers and Guides, the Royal African Regiment, the Ethiopian Regiment, and the Black Brigade.

In January 1776 General George Washington lifted a prohibition against black enlistment in the Continental Army and opened the ranks to free black men. Some colonies also allowed slaves to win their freedom by serving the American forces. About 5,000 blacks fought for the patriot cause.

The American Revolution and the French Revolution of 1789 ignited the freedom movement in Haiti (Saint Domingue). Led in 1791 by a Jamaican known as Boukman (because he always carried a book) and François-Dominique Toussaint, known as **TOUSSAINT L'OUVERTURE** (circa 1743-1803), slaves and free blacks fought the island's plantation owners and French army for the next two years, until slavery was abolished on September 4, 1793. Boukman was killed in the conflict and Toussaint, a former house slave who had acquired property and some wealth, gained favor with the French army. During the next nine years, Toussaint became commander of the island's army, and he then planned a second revolt. In 1802 he was arrested and shipped to a prison in France where he died from tuberculosis and malnutrition. On January 1, 1804, Toussaint's protégé, Jean-Jacques Dessalines, declared Saint Domingue the independent republic of Haiti.

MEN THAT DARED:
AFRICAN-AMERICAN MILITARY SERVICE

GAIL BUCKLEY

From a personal point of view, writing a book about black soldiers
and learning American history through 225 years of the black military
experience made me a superpatriot; I wanted to wrap myself in the flag and
retire hyphenated-Americanism. However fascinating the history
of 15th- and 16th-century West Africa, the story of 18th- and 19th-century
North America is more to the point and much more exciting. The integrat-
ed ranks of the Continental Army, what Washington called his "mixed
multitude," mean more to me than all of Askia the Great's warriors.

The slave trade aside, African-American history can be said to begin
with the black militiamen of Lexington, Concord, and Bunker Hill.
Thanks to those fighting men, patriotism is one of the great themes of black
history. Crispus Attucks, first martyr of the Revolution and centerpiece
of Paul Revere's "Bloody Massacre" broad sheet of March 12, 1770, was not
only a fugitive slave, he was also a symbol of resistance to tyranny. "Who
taught the British soldier that he might be defeated?" asked John Hancock.
"Who dared look into his eyes? I place, therefore, this Crispus Attucks in
the foremost rank of the men that dared."

There were other men who "dared," slave and free. I was fortunate to
meet some of their descendants. Barzillai Lew, a French and Indian War
veteran and one of Ethan Allen's Green Mountain Boys at Ticonderoga, was
a fifer-drummer from Massachusetts, who was said to have raised American
morale at Bunker Hill by playing "Yankee Doodle." Adam Pierce, another
French and Indian War veteran and a New Jersey militiaman, fought with
Washington himself at Monmouth Court House—a victory, despite
100-degree-plus heat, barely relieved by "Molly Pitcher" 's jugs of water.

Talking to Lew and Pierce descendants, I learned that members of their
families had served in nearly every American war since the Revolution. They
definitely had a very proprietary sense about America. One female Lew
descendant, who "couldn't be bothered" to join the Daughters of the

American Revolution (DAR), actually had two ancestors at Bunker Hill. (The other married Barzillai's granddaughter.) A Pierce descendant, on the other hand, was one of the very few black DAR members. Her brothers belonged to the Sons of the American Revolution, whose reputation on race was better than that of the Daughters—called "Aryan hussies" by Langston Hughes for their treatment of Marian Anderson.

I stress the historical presence of blacks at America's birth because it is part of what made me a patriot. This land, in spirit and fact, is our land too—it's our birthright. There is even a founding African-American family: Antonio and Isabella, two of the famous "20 negars" received from a Dutch man-of-war by John Rolfe in 1619 Jamestown in exchange for food. By 1619 the African slave trade was nearly 200 years old and flourishing in Central and South America, but Antonio and Isabella, like English convicts, were held in indentured servitude rather than lifetime slavery. When Indians attacked Jamestown in 1622, and more than 300 people were killed, including John Rolfe, Antonio and Isabella and the colony's other blacks were conspicuously spared in the carnage. This was fortunate for little William Tucker, Antonio and Isabella's son, who became, in 1624, the first child of African parents to be baptized in North America.

It's no accident that the American Revolution may be the only revolution not followed by a reign of terror. All revolutions are about socio-economics, geography, and politics, but the American Revolution was also about principles and a new multiform concept of freedom: freedom from church, king, and political tyranny; freedom of thought, voice, and vote; and, most revolutionary of all, freedom to pursue happiness. Black Americans heard the message too. As inhabitants of the country, they believed that the right to pursue freedom and happiness should also belong to them. If the ultimate duty of patriotism, as many Americans believe, is pushing one's country to live up to its highest ideals, then black veterans, who have always pushed, have always been patriots. James Forten, a black Revolutionary powder-boy, taken prisoner by the British, walked home barefoot to Philadelphia after the war and became one of the richest and most activist black men in America. He spoke out against the Fugitive Slave Law of 1793 and the American Colonization Society of 1817 (which sought to transport free blacks to Liberia), and in 1833, with William Lloyd Garrison, founded the American Anti-Slavery Society. "Those whom liberty has cost nothing, do not know how to prize it," said "Dr. Harris," another black Revolutionary veteran.

If the 18th-century black story is inspiring, then the 19th-century black story is amazing. Giants, black and white, strode the American landscape—including a wartime president who wrote his own magnificent and sublimely eloquent speeches. In a wonderful way, all the giants come together in the story of the 54th Massachusetts—the northern answer to *Gone With the Wind*. Formed in Boston right after Emancipation, the 54th was the abolitionist regiment par excellence—in it were the two sons of Frederick Douglass, as sergeant and sergeant major, and the two younger brothers of William and Henry James, as second lieutenants. George L. Stearns, organizer of the 54th (and secret backer of John Brown's raid), had asked for black officers, but the War Department refused.

In July 1863 the regiment moved from Boston to the South Carolina Sea Islands, first southern foothold of emancipation. There was Col. Robert Gould Shaw, 54th commander and member of Harvard's "Fighting Class" of 1860, and New Bedford seaman Sgt. William Carney, who became the first black winner of the new Medal of Honor. There was even a third set of abolitionist brothers, the Hallowells, known as the "Fighting Quakers." Already based in the Sea Islands, Col. Thomas Wentworth Higginson commanded the ex-slave First South Carolina Volunteers—who, to the outrage of the South and the delight of Lincoln, single-handedly captured Jacksonville, Florida. Harriet Tubman, one of the giants of the century, was a nurse in Clara Barton's Sea Island Union Army base hospital. Every black American in military service has fought two wartime enemies, one of whom always wore an American uniform. The military, like politics, traditionally belonged to southerners because of the slave system's surplus white male population. Thus, American military racism was often of the egregious "what doesn't kill you makes you stronger" school. Some of the greatest black frontline heroes fought the American military establishment itself—namely Henry O. Flipper and Johnson C. Whittaker, et al., who fought their way through West Point in the 19th century.

Bad as 19th-century American racism was, the 20th century, which coincided with the rise of southern revisionism, was far worse. W. E. B. Du Bois called southern revisionism, which began in 1876 when Federal troops protecting black voters were removed from the South, "one of the most stupendous efforts the world ever saw to discredit human beings, an effort involving universities, history, social life and religion." Eventually it erased all black heroism from history, replacing it with the myth of the happy slave.

World Wars I and II were the most racist wars in American history. An overt racist, President Woodrow Wilson retired Col. Charles Young, America's highest-ranking black officer, at the onset of the First World War so he couldn't become a general. Wilson kept seasoned black Buffalo Soldier troops out of the war, too. They had fought Indians, Cubans, and Filipinos, but weren't permitted to fight white Europeans. He "gave" black American combat troops to the French, to fight in French uniform under the French flag, because he didn't want blacks to bear arms for America. Nevertheless, these lightly trained draftee and National Guard regiments, such as New York's 369th Regiment (the Harlem Hell-Fighters), became the most highly decorated and longest fighting Americans in the war. Sgt. Henry Johnson of the 369th, a New York Central redcap in peacetime, became the first World War I American to win the Croix de Guerre.

Any black American who served in World War I or II deserves a medal for valor above and beyond the call of duty, in the face of American military racism. The anger and humiliation that most black men carried throughout the Second World War often made it impossible for them to speak about their experiences to their families. For searing testimonials, I recommend

The Invisible Soldier, Mary Penick Motley's first-person World War II interviews. For my book, *American Patriots,* I was lucky to be able to meet some of the extraordinary men and women who made World War II military history: the first black men in the Air Corps, Marine Corps, Armored Corps, Navy officer corps—and the first women in uniform. Despite egregious racism, all were openly proud of their military records and experiences. They are some of the most confident people I have ever met. They knew how good they had to be to get where they were. They are fairly called the greatest generation.

The best thing about my research was discovering literary veterans. Elizabeth Keckley, author of *Behind the Scenes,* wasn't a veteran, but she was a Civil War White House eyewitness. As Mary Todd Lincoln's seamstress and closest confidant, Keckley wrote a tell-all best-seller about the sad, kind, praying President and the unstable and extravagant First Lady. Henry O. Flipper described his personal U.S. Military Academy wars in *The Colored Cadet at West Point.* Walter Stevens, author of *Chip on My Shoulder,* was a veteran of the Spanish-American War. Enlisting in patriotic fervor at the age of 16, he grew up to become an entrepreneur and civil rights activist. "Force, and a healthy hatred for oppression," he wrote in 1946, "will do more to settle the colored man's problem than anything else."

Addie Hunton and Kathryn Johnson, authors of *Two Colored Women with the American Expeditionary Forces,* were YMCA workers, not veterans, but they vividly reported World War I racism from the ground up. World War I veteran Harry Haywood, author of *Black Bolshevik,* was so furious at military racism that he joined his older brother in the Communist Party. On the other hand, the black veterans of the Spanish Civil War, in which black and white Americans fought side by side for the first time since the Revolution, were the happiest veterans I met. They were fighting the good fight against fascism, and there was no racism in Spain. James Yates and Vaughn Love, two literary veterans of the Abraham Lincoln Brigade, became my friends. Yates, a peripatetic octogenarian, sold copies of his memoir *From Mississippi to Madrid* on the streets of Greenwich Village. Vaughn Love, son of a World War I Army doctor and godson of Sgt. Henry Johnson, the World War I hero, wrote an unpublished memoir of his life in Spain and World War II. Cited for conspicuous bravery at Spain's Battle for Brunete, Love went on to join the segregated Quartermaster Corps and land at Normandy's Red Dog Beach on D Day.

Other memorable World War II memoirs were Nelson Peery's *Black Fire,* on the 93rd Division; Bill Downey's *Uncle Sam Must Be Losing the War,* on the first black Marines; Carl Rowan's *Breaking Barriers,* on becoming one of the first black Navy officers; Gen. Benjamin O. Davis, Jr.'s *Benjamin O. Davis, Jr.: American,* on the first black pilots; and Charity Adams's *One Woman's Army,* on the first black WACs. David Parks's *GI Diary* was a memoir of Vietnam. And Gen. Colin L. Powell's *My American Journey* reflected both Vietnam and the Gulf War. Powell, of course, helped create the New Army, whose zenith was the Gulf War, representing the last stage in the long journey from most racist of public entities to least—with heroes of all races and both sexes.

The black military experience not only made me believe in my country, it made me believe in the military ethos for men and women of all ages. The veterans I met are among the best people I have ever known. "All the hunters, gatherers, defenders, knights, samurais, and swordsmen," wrote Franciscan priest Richard Rohr, "are, in fact, telling us something good about focus, determination, and courage for the common good." Every civil rights hero, in or out of uniform, from Crispus Attucks to Frederick Douglass to Harriet Tubman to Rosa Parks to Martin Luther King, is an example of "focus, determination, and courage for the common good." We betray their struggle whenever we don't bother to vote or don't bother to defend the Constitution when it's in jeopardy. "I live in this country," said St. Louis fire captain Garland Ambus in a December 2001 *Crisis* maga- zine article on patriotism. "I don't think there's another country where I want to live. You just have to keep going and keep fighting until it's fair." Fighting to make America true to its own "patriot dreams" is surely one of the highest forms of national service.

BUFFALO SOLDIERS, 25TH INFANTRY, CIRCA 1890, FORT KEOGH, MONTANA

For more than 25 years the Buffalo Soldiers not only engaged in battles with Indians, but they built forts and escorted wagon trains, mail stages, and railroad crews. They mapped and charted areas and located sources of water. Black soldiers were responsible for opening millions of square miles of western lands to peaceful settlement and development.

*Born a slave in Ulster County, New York,
Sojourner Truth arrived in New York
City in 1829, where she worked as a domestic. Transformed by a mystical experience
in 1843, she changed her name and began
traveling as a preacher and abolitionist. Truth
was also a staunch champion of the women's-
rights movement.*

Manumission, Anti-Slavery, and Abolition

Individuals who purchased, inherited, or acquired slaves through other means had the right to set them free. Some exercised this right, granting freedom to individual enslaved Africans as well as to groups. Individuals were sometimes awarded their freedom as a reward for some good deed they had done for their owners, including informing on rebellious slaves. Some negotiated deals in which they would be granted their freedom if they earned a certain amount of money within a prescribed period of time. Some owners freed their enslaved African concubines and/or the children they had sired with them. Some freed elderly and infirm Africans so as to rid themselves of the burden of supporting them. Still others freed individuals or their entire slave populations in their wills at the time of their deaths. These acts of manumission were documented through wills and manumission papers, since the relationships between the owners and the enslaved Africans were both legal and economic.

Though individuals owned the vast majority of enslaved Africans, some were purchased by municipal and other government entities. In New York, for instance, the village of New Amsterdam owned one of the earliest allotments of slaves brought to the colony. The colony, like other owners, could and did manumit its "property." Slavery in the Americas derived its legal status from local, colonial, and metropolitan governments. Since it was written into the laws that governed Europe's colonies in the Americas during the earliest stages of colonization, and constantly revised throughout the period of slavery, it would take acts of these various levels of government to abolish the institution.

Slavery had been a system of labor organization and management in the Americas for more than a hundred years when the British established their first permanent colony in 1607. It did not become legally entrenched in the British colonies until the mid-1660s. The 13 British colonies that would eventually become the United States were therefore among the last societies to adopt slavery as a dominant system of labor. Nevertheless, slavery was almost universally accepted as right and just in the Atlantic world prior to the 1780s. The Quakers published a manifesto condemning slavery in 1688, and in 1775 they organized the first abolition society in the United States. During the colonial period, however, only the enslaved Africans consistently

SAMUEL CORNISH (1795-1858)
Born of free parents in Sussex County, Delaware, Cornish organized the New Demeter Street Presbyterian Church in New York City, where he was ordained. With John Russwurm, he established Freedom's Journal *in 1827, the first black newspaper in the United States, and was also editor of the* Colored American, *founded by Philip Bell in 1837.*

JOHN BROWN (1800-1859)
In the spring of 1858, Brown convened a meeting of blacks and whites in Ontario, Canada, at which he announced his plan to establish in the Maryland and Virginia mountains a stronghold for escaping slaves. A year later, with an armed band of 16 whites and 5 blacks, Brown took over the federal arsenal at Harpers Ferry. Hoping that escaped slaves would join his rebellion and form an "army of emancipation," Brown was subdued with his supporters two days later by the U.S. military. Overpowered, Brown himself was wounded, and ten of his followers (including two sons) were killed. He was tried for murder, slave insurrection, and treason against the state and was convicted and hanged.

1, *front*   1, *reverse*   2   3   4

Above:

ABOLITION COINS

1. *Liberty Proclaimed to the Captives, 1834. On the coin's reverse side: "Is not this the fast that I have chosen? To loose the hands of wickedness. To undo the heavy burdens and to let the oppressed go free, and that ye break every yoke? Isaiah 58:6." Metal.*

2. *Slavery Abolished by Great Britain, 1834.*

3. *"Am I Not a Woman and a Sister?" On the coin's reverse side: "To the Friends of Justice, Mercy, and Freedom." Metal.*

4. *Freedom Without Slavery, circa 1850. A copper halfpenny with a rum or molasses barrel on the front and a cotton bale on the reverse side of the coin, believed by numismatists to have been minted by Barbados merchant Moses Tolanto. An 1816 slave rebellion in Barbados signaled the eventual end of slavery, which was abolished there and throughout the British West Indies in 1834.*

called for the abolition of slavery through word and deed. The first and most consistent abolitionists were those enslaved Africans who said slavery was wrong. Fueled by the ideological currents of the French and American Revolutions, opponents of slavery in Pennsylvania, New York, Massachusetts, and Virginia established manumission societies urging the freeing of slaves by will or deed. By 1826 there were 143 manumission societies in the United States, 103 of them in the South. During this period, a number of states passed laws mandating a gradual abolition of slavery. The federal government of the United States was one of the last nations to abolish it.

Beginning in the 1830s, opponents of slavery in the United States began to call for its complete and immediate abolition. Prior to the Civil War, upward of 200,000 Americans joined various anti-slavery and abolition societies and waged vigorous ideological and political campaigns against it. Black abolitionists, many of them fugitives, played leading roles in building the case against slavery. When Abraham Lincoln was elected President of the United States on an anti-slavery platform, South Carolina withdrew from the Union and triggered the start of the Civil War.

In the meantime, newly independent nations and more enlightened European colonial powers abolished slavery and the slave trade throughout the Americas. Haiti abolished slavery in 1783. Argentina (1813); Colombia (1814); Central America (1824); New York State (1827); and the West Indies (1834) all abolished slavery before Lincoln issued his Emancipation Proclamation (1863), which freed only slaves in Southern states that were part of the Confederacy. Only the passage of the 13th Amendment (1865) after the Civil War ended slavery in the United States.

THE NEGRO'S COMPLAINT.

Forc'd from home and all its pleasures,
   Afric's coast I left forlorn;
To increase a stranger's treasures,
   O'er the raging billows borne.
Men from England* bought and sold me,
   Paid my price in paltry gold;
But though slave they have enroll'd me,
   Minds are never to be sold.

Still in thought as free as ever—
   What are England's rights (I ask)
Me from my delights to sever,
   Me to torture, me to task?
Fleecy locks and black complexion
   Cannot forfeit Nature's claim;
Skins may differ, but affection
   Dwells in White and Black the same.

Why did all-creating Nature
   Make the Plant for which we toil,
Sighs must fan it, tears must water,
   Sweat of ours must dress the soil.
Think, ye Masters iron-hearted,
   Lolling at your jovial boards,
Think how many backs have smarted
   For the sweets your Cane affords.

Is there, as ye sometimes tell us—
   Is there ONE who reigns on high?
Has HE bid you buy and sell us—
   Speaking from his throne, the sky?

Ask Him if your knotted scourges,
   Fetters, blood-extorting screws,
Are the means which duty urges
   Agents of his will to use?

Hark! He answers—Wild tornadoes,
   Strewing yonder sea with wrecks,
Wasting towns, plantations, meadows,
   Are the voice with which He speaks.
He, foreseeing what vexation,
   Afric's sons would undergo,
Fixed their tyrants' habitation
   Where his whirlwind answers—"No!"

By our blood in Afric wasted,
   Ere our necks receiv'd the chain—
By the miseries which we tasted,
   Crossing in your barks the main—
By our sufferings, since ye brought us
   To the man-degrading mart,
All sustain'd with patience, taught us
   Only by a broken heart—

Deem our nation brutes no longer,
   Till some reason ye shall find
Worthier to regard, and stronger
   Than the *color* of our kind!
Slaves of Gold! whose sordid dealings
   Tarnish all your boasted powers,
Prove that *ye* have human feelings,
   Ere ye proudly question ours.

He that stealeth a man and selleth him, or if he be found in his hand, he shall surely be put to death. Exodus xxi. 16.
* ENGLAND had 800,000 Slaves, and she has made them FREE. America has 2,250,000!—and she HOLDS THEM FAST!!!

Sold at the American Anti-Slavery Offic , 143 Nassau Street, New-York.

ANTI-SLAVERY COMMEMORATIVES

AM I NOT A MAN AND A BROTHER? became the most famous symbol of the 19th-century abolitionist movement. In 1787 the Quaker-endorsed Society for Effecting the Abolition of the Slave Trade commissioned potter Josiah Wedgwood to design a "seal" for the Society's anti-slavery campaign. Fashioned into plates, dishes, snuff boxes, and commemorative medallions, it was also commonly depicted on jewelry, bracelets, cameos, and hair ornaments. Though it advertised the fight against slavery, the design portrayed enslaved blacks as noble savages pleading for the help of white abolitionists.

Left: **THE NEGRO'S COMPLAINT, CIRCA 1850**
American Anti-Slavery Society broadside.

Below: **"AM I NOT A MAN," WEDGWOOD CLAY POTTERY, ENGLAND, CIRCA 1840**
Commemorative plate with the popular abolitionist statement and symbol.

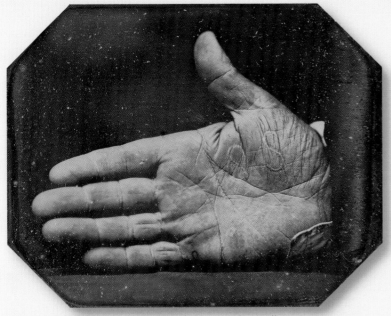

Branded hand of Capt. Jonathan Walker

The dramatic and powerful testimony of former slaves, runaways, and abolitionists who had assisted slaves benefited the anti-slavery cause. In 1844 **CAPT. JONATHAN WALKER** became a national hero when he aided seven fugitive slaves trying to escape to freedom in the Bahamas. Though all were caught and jailed in Pensacola, Walker stood trial and pleaded not guilty on the grounds that "assisting men to escape from slavery was not a crime." Walker's punishment included 11 months in jail and the branding of his right hand— with a red hot iron pressed onto the ball of his hand for about 20 seconds—to signify SS, or "slave stealer."

In upstate Cazenovia, NY, near several Underground Railroad routes that passed northward to Canada, an anti-slavery gathering in 1850 (opposite) attracted 2,000 people. Organized in response to the new Fugitive Slave Act, which levied heavy fines against anyone who aided runaways and gave federal marshals jurisdiction as slave catchers in free states, the convention featured fugitive **FREDERICK DOUGLASS** (1818-1895), seated in front of abolitionist Gerrit Smith, and sisters Mary and Emily Edmondson, wearing plaid shawls. The sisters were among 14 siblings born into slavery in Washington, D.C. Their freedom was purchased by Rev. Henry Ward Beecher and his Plymouth Church in Brooklyn, which raised money to buy the young women and spare them from being sold into prostitution. Their case caught the attention of Beecher's sister, Harriet Beecher Stowe, then writing **Uncle Tom's Cabin**. Douglass, the most famous runaway, escaped from slavery in Maryland in 1838, fleeing to New York via train and boats.

Founded in Philadelphia on December 4, 1833, the American Anti-Slavery Society was modeled after the Anti-Slavery Society, which was established in England in the 1780s and had succeeded in abolishing slavery in the British colonies. The Society advocated the immediate abolition of slavery, sponsored tours of white and black orators, and published millions of copies of anti-slavery tracts, pamphlets, books, and newspapers, including the **DECLARATION OF THE ANTI-SLAVERY CONVENTION**, December 4, 1833 (below).

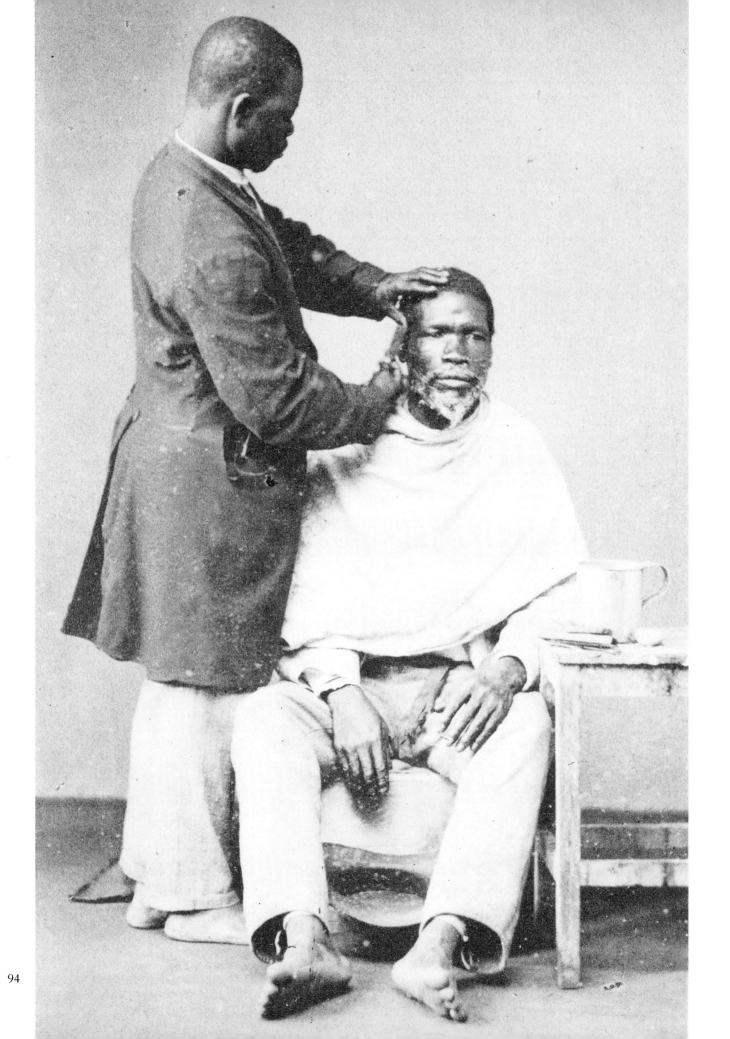

From Property to Property Ownership

Legally, slavery in the Americas was first and foremost a property relationship: Enslaved Africans were legally (though unjustly) the property of
their owners. As a consequence, they were bought and sold on the open
market, used as collateral in business transactions, hired out to private and
public users, given away as gifts of esteem, taxed based on their value
in the marketplace, and counted as part of the real property of estates when
their owners died. Upon arrival in the Americas, they owned nothing, not
even themselves.

Slave societies repeatedly passed laws prohibiting blacks from accumulat-
ing property or participating in money making activities on their own
behalf. At the same time, these very laws documented the fact that enslaved
Africans were very actively involved in acquiring and selling goods and
services as well as becoming property owners and at times major players in
the moneyed economy. Enslaved men and women who worked in gold,
silver, and diamond mines kept some of these nuggets and gems for themselves and traded them on the black market. Those who had been stolen and
sold to their owners were accused of stealing from their owners and were
severely punished if caught. Those who were not caught, sold or traded their
valuable commodities and used the returns to buy clothing and other ameni-
ties, gifts for loved ones, and their own or loved ones' freedom.

On plantations throughout the Americas, enslaved Africans were allotted
parcels of land to grow food to supplement their own and their owners'
diets. Enterprising individuals and families turned these plots, which frequently became tracts of several acres, into privately held farms, which they
worked after hours and on weekends. In addition to their own dietary
supplements, they grew foodstuffs for sale, raised pigs and cattle for sale, and
at times even raised their own tobacco, cotton, rice, and other cash crops.
These they either sold directly to their owners or sold or traded on the
open market. Laws prohibiting this activity were largely ineffective, and as a
consequence, many enterprising enslaved Africans earned enough to accumulate wealth, acquire property, and buy back ownership in themselves and
their families.

Runaways and maroons, who were branded criminals and outlaws for
stealing themselves, carried out periodic raids on plantations and towns,

Above:
**MARKET WOMEN, CIRCA 1880,
BRAZIL, ALBUMEN PRINT**

Opposite:
**PORTRAITS OF MEN,
CIRCA 1870, BRAZIL**
*While "earning slaves" in Brazil lived indepen-
dently in towns and cities, they turned a portion
of their wages over to their owners, some of
whom were poor and depended entirely on this
income. The earning slaves worked as barbers,
market vendors, porters, cooks, and nursemaids.
Many eventually purchased their freedom.*

Right:
AFRICAN HOUSE

An example of African-influenced architecture, this house was owned by African-American plantation owner Marie Therese Coin-Coin Metoyer (1742-1816). A former slave, Metoyer raised cattle and grew vegetables on her 1,000-acre plantation, located on Louisiana's Cane River.

Opposite:
TOM MOLINEAUX (1784-1818)

Born a slave in the District of Columbia, Molineaux was the property of his master until he won his freedom and $100 by defeating a slave from a neighboring plantation in a boxing match. He traveled to London, where he became the first American to fight in an international bout. Although he lost two matches with British champion Tom Cribbs at the peak of his career, he holds the distinction of being America's first great boxer.

Opposite (overlay):
PROMISSORY NOTE, DECEMBER 30, 1843

Document verifying hire for $63 of a slave woman and her three children for the year 1844

taking with them food stores, livestock, and other goods. Runaway slave notices indicate that these fugitives from injustice frequently carried with them valuable and distinctive property items.

Individuals who mastered certain crafts were hired out by their owners for short- and long-term periods. Owners could make up to 20 percent profit per year on the price for a skilled slave's work, but these skilled laborers also expected to make extra compensation for themselves. Between 60,000 and 160,000 enslaved Africans were hired out each year in the American South during the antebellum period. They earned from five dollars to twenty dollars per month for themselves, depending on the kind of work they did. They, too, used their earnings to acquire property and buy back their freedom.

Meanwhile, free blacks in both the North and South created and operated businesses, purchased homes and other real estate, and, in places such as Louisiana and South Carolina, even owned and ran slave plantations. After the Civil War, blacks rushed to entrust their savings to the Freedman's Bank. By 1872, seven years after the end of the Civil War, some 70,000 depositors throughout the United States had made deposits totaling over three million dollars. After the failure of the Freedman's Bank under white leadership and management, blacks established and ran their own banks, building and loan associations, real estate companies, and retail enterprises. Today, descendants of propertyless slaves hold billions of dollars in assets and an annual purchasing power greater than the national debt of many countries.

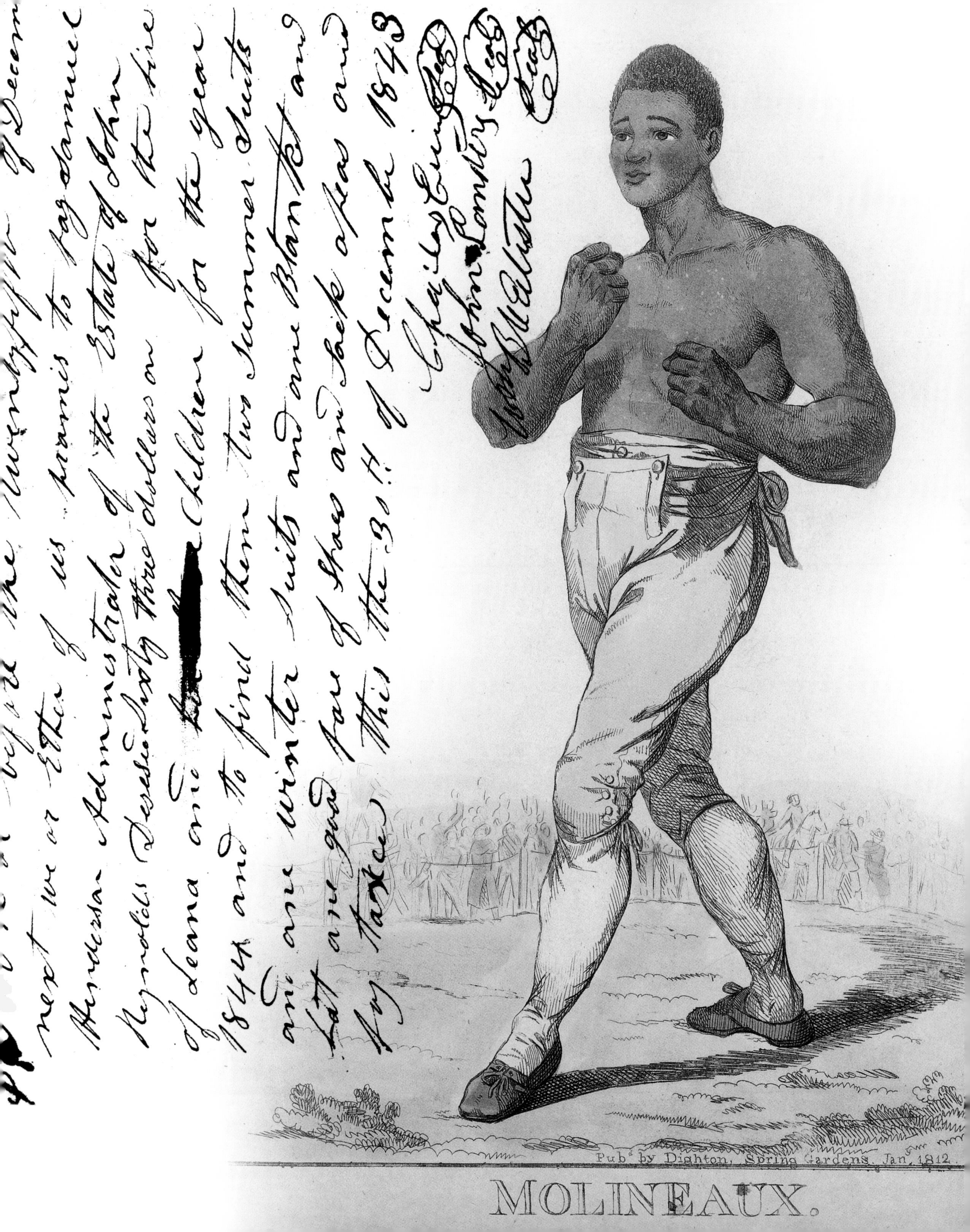
before the twentyfifth of Decem
next we or Ether of us promis to pay Samuel
Henderson Administrater of the Estate of John
Reynolds Desesed Sixty three dollars on for the hire
of Leana and [redacted] Children for the year
1844 and to find them two Summer Suits
and one Winter Suits and one Blanket and
hat one good pare of Shoes and Sack a peas and
pay taxes this the 30th of December 1843
Charles Ewing Seal
John Lowdry Seal
John B McAlister Seal
Pubd by Dighton, Spring Gardens, Jany 1812
MOLINEAUX.

CLAIMING OWNERSHIP OF ONESELF

Self-emancipation or "claiming ownership of oneself" took many forms during the slavery era. Worst for slave owners were runaways, whose flight to freedom left them uncompensated for their loss of "property." Slaves who were able to hire themselves out after their own work hours were often able to save enough money to buy their own freedom or freedom for others.

ABSALOM JONES (1746-1818) was born a slave in Delaware. In 1762 his mother, five brothers, and sister were sold, and Jones was taken to Philadelphia, where during the day he worked in a store and at night he attended a school for blacks. In 1770 he married a slave and then bought her freedom, six years before purchasing his own. In 1787 Jones joined **RICHARD ALLEN** in forming the Free African Society. The founding pastor of the African Church of Philadelphia (renamed in 1794 the Saint Thomas African Episcopal Church) in 1808, he informally established January 1 (the date on which the U.S. slave trade ended) as a day of thanksgiving and celebration, creating an alternative holiday to the Fourth of July for African Americans.

PIERRE TOUSSAINT (circa 1766-1853) was born a slave in Saint Domingue (Haiti). Toussaint came to New York City with his white owner, who fled from the Haitian revolution. A hairdresser to many of the city's wealthiest women, Toussaint, who was freed by his owner upon her death in 1807, earned enough money to purchase the freedom of several of his family members. Famous for his philanthropy, he supported many charities and donated much of his fortune to aiding orphans.

BLANCHE KELSO BRUCE (1841-1898) was born a slave in rural Virginia. Learning to read and write from a tutor who was hired to educate his master's son, Bruce escaped from slavery during the Civil War and settled in Hannibal, Missouri, where he organized the state's first school for blacks. In 1869 he moved to Mississippi and organized 21 schools, though all were segregated, for black and white students. Known as a self-help advocate—a reputation that made him popular among blacks and whites—in 1874 he became the first African American elected to a full six-year term in the U.S. Senate. Appointed Registrar of the Treasury by President Garfield in 1881, Bruce was the first African American with his signature on U.S. currency. He later became a lecturer and board member of Howard University.

Absalom Jones

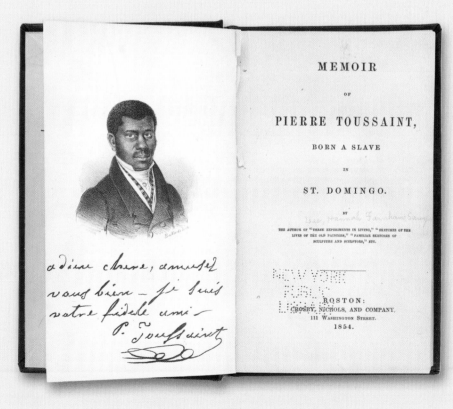

FREEDMEN IN NICODEMUS, KANSAS, 1885

The first great wave of African-American migration begin in 1877, just as Reconstruction was ending in the South. In the next two years over 20,000 blacks migrated from Southern states to Kansas. Pioneers in the Kansas Fever Exodus of 1879, they became known as the "Exodusters." In Nicodemus, Kansas, seven hundred blacks established a promising prairie town with stores, schools, churches, farms, businesses and homes. Enduring harsh weather, struggling crops, and cattle barons who trampled their land, Nicodemus was unable to survive the devastating news that the Union Pacific Railroad would bypass the town. Instead the railroad connected to a nearby white village and the town dwindled—an experience shared by many black towns that failed to attract a rail line.

A NEW PEOPLE

pañol con India,
Mestizo.

Mestizo con Española
Castizo.

Castizo con Española
Español.

Español con Mora
Mulato.

5

6

7

Mulato con Española,
Morisco.

Morisco con Española
Chino.

Chino con India.
Salta atas.

Salta atas con Mulata
Lobo.

9

10

11

1

Lobo con China
Gibaro.

Gibaro con Mulata
Albarazado

Albarazado con Negra
Canbujo.

Canbujo con India
Sanbaigo.

13

14

15

CHAPTER 4

A NEW PEOPLE

The overwhelming majority of people of African descent in the United States are descended from enslaved Africans. Variously named negros, *piesas,* or simply Africans, they were, in fact, representatives of an extraordinarily diverse African population taken principally from selected regions of West Africa. Most came from a broad region along the Atlantic coast of Africa stretching from modern Ghana and Nigeria through the Bights of Benin and Biafra. Or they came from modern-day Congo and Angola. Still others came from today's Sierra Leone, Guinea, and Senegal, and regions of Africa's west coast interior. They were Mandingo and Bambara, Igbo and Kongo, Akan and Ibibio. Yoruba, Ewe, Fon, and Allada-speaking people from the Bight of Benin were relatively few, but Kikongo, Bakongo, Kimbandu, and other Bantu-speaking peoples were more numerous. Drawn from diverse African societies, speaking diverse African languages, practicing equally diverse traditional African religions as well as Islam, the initial enslaved African immigrants who populated the United States in the 17th and 18th centuries were as much strangers to each other as they were to their European captors.

During the first 200 years of slavery, however, they transformed themselves into a new people—a new African-American people. Ethnic and religious boundaries faded as African men and women established new conjugal and familial relationships across these barriers. Sharply drawn racial categories adopted in the United States grouped people based on their skin color, hair texture, and other presumed racial characteristics. All Africans, regardless of their ethnic or religious backgrounds, were transformed into a single black racial group. Laws and official policy notwithstanding, the black group, the new African-American people, became an even more complex people biologically, ethnically, and racially. In addition to the one or more African ethnicities, Europeans of all types and Native Americans of diverse ethnic and national backgrounds were included in the genetic makeup of these new African-American peoples. Among the most remarkable consequences of the enslaved African experience in the United States is that they transformed themselves and were transformed into a cohesive racial group—

Above:

THE CITY OF BENIN, 1686

The 17th-century image of Benin in present day Nigeria depicts the capital city of a vast empire. By the mid-16th century, the empire stretched from the region of northern Lagos to the Niger River Delta. Presided over by the Oba, or king, the city was both a major trading center and religious and political capital for the Edo people of Nigeria.

Opposite:

RACIAL MIXTURE IN MEXICO, CIRCA 1870

The caste painting indicates the variety of "new people"—mixtures of European, African, and natives—after three centuries of colonization and slavery in Mexico. Artist: Unknown.

Preceding pages:

Street performers in the streets of Salvador, Bahia, Brazil, practice capoëra, a form of martial arts. Capoëra developed as a clever way for African slaves in Brazil to disguise their martial arts training; to plantation owners, it looked like merry dancing.

**DETAILS FROM AN ETCHING SHOW-
ING DIFFERENT ETHNIC GROUPS
(BENGUELA/ ANGOLA/ CONGO/
MONJOLO), CIRCA 1835**

*Enslaved Africans were transported to the
Americas during the slave trade and came from
many different ethnic groups, primarily on
the western coast of Africa. It should be noted,
however, that the labels in Rugendas's drawings
(Cabinda/Quiloa/Rebolla/Mina) refer
to these Africans' points of departure from along
the coast of Africa rather than to any ethnic
or religious group. Mina, for example, takes its
name from Elmina Castle, a Portuguese-built
fortress and slave-trading headquarters on
the Gold Coast of West Africa, which exported
enslaved Africans. Artist: Johann Moritz
Rugendas. Lithograph: Pierre-Roch Vigneron.
Published in* Voyage Pittoresque et
Historique au Brésil, *Paris.*

new American people. In other parts of the Americas, racial, ethnic, and/or biological mixtures were used to create elaborate and distinctive group identities reflecting these mixtures. In the United States the one-drop rule prevailed. The known existence of a single African ancestor in one's family tree (one drop of black blood) consigned one to the black racial group. In the United States, black/white mixtures such as mulattos, quadroons, and octoroons all formed a part of the black group unless they were white enough to "pass"—disappear into the white group. As a consequence, African Americans, the black racial group, likely includes representatives of all the people of the United States in its genetic makeup.

The new African-American people were more than simply biologically and genetically transformed peoples. In the context of slavery, they invented a new African-American slave culture. In the place of the diverse African languages they brought with them, they invented new languages to communicate with each other and their colonial masters. One of a special group of New World African languages created by enslaved Africans, "black English," is a synthesis of English vocabulary and largely African grammatical structure. Enslaved Africans also created new, uniquely American religions, musics, dances, cuisines, and art forms.

It was within the confines of the slave quarters that enslaved Africans of diverse backgrounds created their new social relations and cultural forms. In the context of the most oppressive and dehumanizing conditions on the plantation, they formulated new rules of ethical and moral behavior and fostered cooperation and mutual assistance among themselves in order to survive and affirm their own identities, values, and ideals. It was in the quarters that they created new family and social relationships. It was in the quarters that they affirmed their faith in God and their love for one another. The more they developed and affirmed their unique cultural values and practices the better they were able to resist the power and control of whites.

The sense of group solidarity developed in the quarters encouraged enslaved Africans to unite to protect themselves from slavery's most dehumanizing practices. The new culture they invented fostered self-esteem, courage, and confidence in the individuals and the group.

Beyond the quarters, another group of African peoples contributed to the development of African-American people and African-American culture. Described variously as "free negroes," "free blacks," or "quasi free negroes," this class of Africans were themselves uniquely American creations. The vast majority of them were former slaves or descendants of slaves. Anomalies in a racially based slave society, where only whites were supposed to be free and where all blacks were supposed to be enslaved, these African men and women and their descendants had escaped slavery through a variety of means. Some had been set free by their slave owners either during the owners' lifetimes or in their wills at death. Others were enterprising, skilled former slaves who earned enough money (although it was often illegal to do so) to buy their own and their families' freedom. Still others simply ran away.

Above:

THE FIRST COLORED SENATOR AND REPRESENTATIVES, IN THE 41ST AND 42ND CONGRESS OF THE UNITED STATES, 1872

(Left to right) Senator Hiram Revels of Mississippi, Representatives Benjamin Turner of Alabama, Robert DeLarge of South Carolina, Josiah Walls of Florida, Jefferson Long of Georgia, Joseph Rainey and Robert B. Elliot of South Carolina. In January 1870 Revels was elected to the U.S. Senate to fill the unexpired term of the former Confederate president, Jefferson Davis. The same year Rainey became the first black elected to the U.S. House of Representatives. Artist: Currier & Ives.

PORTRAIT OF A MAN WITH TRIBAL SCARIFICATION, CIRCA 1860, BAHIA, BRAZIL, ALBUMEN PRINT

These portraits attest to some of the cultural transformations taking place among Africans in Brazil. The Brazilians in these photographs, such as the man wearing a shirt made from a sugar sack, have kept some of their past identity. Cultural changes—religious, physical, linguistic, and otherwise—took place among enslaved Africans as they adapted to their new lives in the Americas and the Caribbean.
Photographer: unknown.

But they were more than that to both enslaved Africans and slave owners. For most enslaved Africans, they were the embodiment of the ideal of black freedom that they aspired to—affirmations of the fact that African peoples were not by their nature destined to always and only be slaves. For slave owners, their very existence threatened the foundations of their racially based slave societies, representing as they did subversive alternative ideals of human existence for their enslaved property. As a consequence, "free blacks," who had been an unwanted presence in slave societies in the United States since the 17th century, were encouraged, and at times forced, to leave the cities and states in which they lived. They were discriminated against in every way and denied the basic human and civil rights accorded white immigrants no matter how recently they had come to the city, state, or country. They were constant victims of policies and vilification campaigns to "keep them in their place."

PORTRAITS OF WOMEN, CIRCA 1880, BAHIA, BRAZIL
Women in traditional clothes sell fruit from their baskets.

Nevertheless, despite attempts to drive them out of their adopted cities, states, and country by legal and extralegal means, the free black population had grown from 59,000 in 1790 to some 488,000 by 1860. Forty-four percent still lived in the South, while 46 percent lived in the North. The advance guard in the development of African-American organizational life during the era of slavery, they established the foundations of the major African-American religious, civic, literary, educational, fraternal, and social organizations during the late 18th and early 19th centuries. They established and owned businesses and other property, were leaders of anti-slavery and abolitionist movements, and were pioneers in a variety of literacy, artistic, scientific, and cultural pursuits. Virtually all of them were little more than a generation removed from slavery. But they were part of the ongoing process of social and cultural change that transformed enslaved African immigrants into a new African-American people.

Through a process of adapting traditional African cultural forms, blending them with the resources found in Euro-American and Native American cultures, enslaved Africans laid the foundation of African-American culture. In so doing, they also Africanized American culture.

EMANCIPATED SLAVES, WHITE AND COLORED, CIRCA 1863

Perhaps more surprising to whites than to blacks were the variety of shades and hues of African Americans, many of whom chose to "pass" for white. Those pictured are all described as attending a New Orleans school for "emancipated slaves," and some "show not the slightest trace of negro blood."

A BOTTOMLESS VITALITY

Discussions of the family life of enslaved Africans usually begin with the fact that slave marriages seldom enjoyed legal status in American society. They continue by recounting incidents of rape and forced liaisons between enslaved men and women. Such discussions also inevitably turn to the degree of family disruption occasioned by the sheer economic functioning of slave societies in which enslaved Africans were chattel—owned, and if necessary or desired, sold by their "masters."

There is abundant evidence that families of enslaved Africans were routinely broken up when members were sold and transported to other plantations or more distant locations. Husbands or wives were sold without regard for their marital status. Children were sold away from parents to raise needed revenue. During the antebellum period, children in the upper South, especially young men, were prime candidates for sale in the domestic slave trade. Slave owners in the upper South frequently forced young men and women to enter sexual liaisons for the express purpose of breeding slaves for the domestic slave trade.

Enslaved African women were also frequently the objects of white male lasciviousness. Slaveholders and their male children, white drivers and overseers, as well as white men in urban settings sought the sexual favors of enslaved African women, and when they were not freely given, resorted to rape to quell their sexual passions. Marital relations between enslaved African men and women were constantly threatened by their lack of legal standing and the unequal power relationships that existed between whites and blacks. The social and political realities of slavery made it virtually impossible for slave husbands and fathers to defend and protect their wives and children without facing severe and often deadly repercussions. Slavery disrupted family life among enslaved Africans and subverted their attempts to normalize their relationships with one another in their new political and cultural settings.

What is largely unstated, and all too frequently underappreciated, is the degree to which African peoples invented whatever family life they enjoyed

Opposite, and above:
MARITCHA LYONS AND HER SISTER, MARY, CIRCA 1865
Maritcha Lyons, daughter of Albro Lyons, a prosperous black New York City businessman, became a prominent civic leader and educator. In 1897 she and Victoria Earle Matthews co-founded the White Rose Mission, a "Christian, non-sectarian Home for Colored Girls and Women, where they may be trained in the principles of practical self-help and right living." The organization greeted boats at Manhattan piers and provided meals and lodging for migrants from the South and the West Indies.

In 1825 free blacks began to purchase land plots in a region of Manhattan that became known as Seneca Village, a predominantly African-American community. In 1842 black merchant Albro Lyons purchased land in the village that included three churches, a school, two cemeteries, and several homes. However, in 1858 Seneca Village was inaccurately termed "rundown and seedy," then condemned and destroyed to make way for the city's new Central Park.

during slavery. Despite the great difficulty that slave families had establishing and maintaining themselves in a system that neither respected nor valued their relationships with one another, enslaved Africans established the foundations of black family life in the quarters and on farms and plantations during slavery.

In Africa the family had been the basis of social organization, including economic and political life. Even in large nation-states and empires, family and kinship networks determined the social and cultural realities of society. Although most of their relationships did not survive the Middle Passage, the concepts of marriage and family did. No longer able, for the most part, to re-create Igbo, Fon, or Akan families because of the diversity of the African populations found in their new American environments, enslaved Africans created new African-American families. Slave men and women from different African ethnic groups forged conjugal bonds and created new family and kinship networks.

Enslaved Africans created their own marriage rituals and ceremonies to consummate their marriages. Slave preachers and religious leaders presided at most of their marriages, but white ministers were also used. Jumping over the broomstick was the most common slave marriage ritual. Sometimes, the prospective bride and groom jumped over the broom three times. At others, each jumped over the other's broom. In still other instances, the woman stood still on one side of the broom while the man jumped over to join her.

Whatever the method of affirming their relationships with one another, the bonds created were as enduring as those created through legal means among whites. Indeed, a study of the 1850 and 1860 manuscript

censuses suggests that a larger percentage of adult slaves compared with southern adult free whites were or had been married at the time of death.

Within the constraints imposed by slavery, slave families carried out the functions of families in all societies. They gave birth to and socialized the young, sustained and nurtured family members, and established and enforced the moral and ethical norms that bound them to one another and to the community. In the quarters, these moral and ethical values were reinforced and sustained by kinship and community networks. Husbands and wives entered into economic relationships, the profits from which were used to buy their freedom. Others simply ran away as a family.

Enslaved Africans frequently married free blacks, who in turn purchased their freedom. Informal conjugal and sacred bonds of relationships were also created between Africans and Native Americans and occasionally whites and Africans or African Americans. By 1860, African-American families included all of these racial and ethnic mixtures. African Americans recognized the difference between ritual marriages and legal marriages. As soon as it was possible to legalize their marriages, they did. Formal and newly legal civil and/or religious marriage ceremonies proliferated during and immediately after the Civil War—so much so that by the second decade after slavery, between 66 and 75 percent of black children lived in two-parent households.

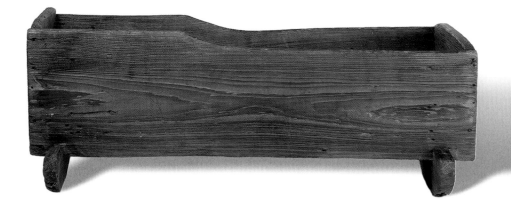

Top:

CRADLE, WOOD, CIRCA 1820

In a slave community elderly women might care for young children or infants in the cradle. However, mothers who were field workers were often expected to keep their infants with them while they worked.

Above:

SLAVE DOLL, COTTON, CIRCA 1850 NORTH CAROLINA

Toys crafted from wood or sewn from old garments were the common playthings for slave children. Children as young as four and five years old were expected to perform daily chores.

Free blacks—former slaves and their descendants—laid the institutional foundations of black life in the Americas during the slavery era. In the United States, where slave preachers and religious leaders had played a major role in establishing independent black religious life, former slaves Richard Allen and James Varick founded the African Methodist Episcopal and African Methodist Episcopal Zion Churches, respectively. Independent black Baptist churches led by slave and free black preachers proliferated throughout the South. A synthesis of European Christian and traditional African religious rituals and practices, these churches became the bases on which African Americans organized their collective social and cultural lives. Free blacks also founded the first black newspapers and political and literary journals during the era of slavery. They used these literary investments to give voice to their own freedom aspirations and to oppose slavery.

The organized, independent political life of African Americans traces its roots back to the National Negro Convention movement of the 1830s. These annual gatherings of free blacks in northern urban areas fashioned collective African-American political agendas, including organized anti-slavery and civil rights campaigns. Enslaved Africans and free blacks established and ran a variety of businesses that served both African Americans and the general public. Restaurants, barbershops, pharmacies, jewelry stores, blacksmith shops, laundries, funeral parlors, and printing and engraving establishments were all founded, owned, and run by black entrepreneurs during the era of slavery. Burial societies founded during the slavery era evolved into black-owned insurance companies. Prince Hall, a former slave from Massachusetts, founded the first Masonic lodge during the 18th century. Numerous literary societies, schools, and social clubs strengthened the institutional infrastructure of African Americans prior to the Civil War. As a consequence, when freedom came, blacks were prepared to assume larger roles in the economic, political, and social life of American society.

Hearth and Home

Keeping marriage and family together was a great struggle for many slaves. Homes and relationships were threatened constantly and could be dissolved in an instant by many factors. The lives of slave owners reverberated profoundly on slaves, and their business and personal interests severely affected slave-family relationships.

A slaveholder's management decisions, economic hardship, marriage, divorce, or death could lead to sale and dispersal of slaves. Word or rumor of a pending sale threatened families and relationships and often gave owners and overseers even greater influence and authority over slaves. Women and teenage girls were especially vulnerable. Threats to sell mothers, fathers, sisters, brothers, sons, and daughters or other family members and friends made enslaved women prone to untoward sexual pressures to influence or stop the sale of a family member.

Injury, sickness, old age, and jealousies could lead also to slave family breakups, as could the normal stresses of family and marriage. Bad behavior and even good behavior threatened the slave family, as model or "excellent" slave boys and girls were commonly given as gifts to friends and family of slaveholders.

Advertisements for slave runaways regularly listed family connections as clues to tracking down fugitives. An 1837 posting in the **Richmond** (Virginia) **Compiler** stated: "He (Joe) ran off without any known cause, and I suppose he is aiming to go to his wife," or as noted in an 1838 **Savannah** (Georgia) **Republican** ad: "It is probable he will aim for Savannah, as he said he had children in that vicinity."

Georgia, Talbot County.

To any ordained Minister of the Gospel, Jewish Rter, Judge, Justice of the Inferior Court, or Justice of the Peace:

YOU ARE HEREBY AUTHORIZED

To join _Charles Gilbert (freedman)_ and

Susan Marshall (freedwoman)

IN THE HOLY STATE OF

MATRIMONY,

According to the Constitution and Laws of this State, and for which this shall be your sufficient License.

Given under my hand and Seal, this _31th_ day of _Dec._ 186_6_

Marion Bethune Ordinary.

Georgia, Talbot County.

I do hereby certify, that _Charles Gilbert freedman_

and _Susan Marshall freedwoman_ were duly joined in

Matrimony, by me, this _27th_ day of _December_ 186_4_

John Pye J. P.

Printed at the Office of the West Georgia Gazette, Talbotton, Ga.

MARHiage

"Jumping the broom"—a traditional slave wedding ceremony in which bride and groom sealed their union by stepping or jumping together over a broom—symbolized matrimonial union and sweeping away of bad spirits in the lives of the new bride and groom. The joyful celebration that brought friends and family together, however, was illegal in slavery states. Slave marriages were disregarded by slave owners who could render any slave marriage or family bond meaningless. Husband and father were irrelevant designations to owners, as the status of slave children was determined solely by the slave status of the mother.

In May 1865 a federal order set "marriage rules" for the legalization of the newly freed slaves "which may be solemnized by any ordained minister of the gospel." By an act of Congress in July 1866, all freemen and women who "shall furnish satisfactory evidence of either their marriage or divorce of all former companions" were declared legally married or eligible for matrimony. States were instructed to license black ministers to perform wedding rites and to provide couples with marriage certificates that carried the text of the law printed on the back.

Opposite: **MARRIAGE CERTIFICATE, DECEMBER 27, 1866**
Marriage certificate of Charles Gilbert and Susan Marshall, Talbot County, Georgia.

Right, top: **MARRIAGE OF A COLORED SOLDIER AT VICKSBURG BY CHAPLAIN WARREN OF THE FREEDMEN'S BUREAU, JUNE 30, 1866, HARPER'S WEEKLY**

HEADQUARTERS, ASSISTANT COMMISSIONER,

BUREAU REFUGEES, FREEDMEN AND ABANDONED LANDS,
South Carolina, Georgia and Florida,
BEAUFORT, S. C., AUG. 11, 1865.

GENERAL ORDERS,
No. 8.

MARRIAGE RULES.

To correct as far as possible one of the most cruel wrongs inflicted by slavery, and also to aid the freedmen in properly appreciating and religiously observing the sacred obligations of the marriage state, the following rules are published for the information and guidance of all connected with this Bureau throughout the States of South Carolina, Georgia and Florida:

SECTION I.

Parties Eligible to Marriage. 1.—All male persons, having never been married, of the age of twenty-one, and all females, having never been married, of the age of eighteen, shall be deemed eligible to marriage.

2.—All married persons who shall furnish satisfactory evidence of either the marriage or divorce of all former companions, according to the usages of slavery, or of their decease, will be eligible to marriage again.

3.—All married persons, producing satisfactory evidence of having been separated from their companions by slavery for a period of three years, and that they have no evidence that they are alive; or, if alive, that they will ever, probably, be restored to them, may be allowed to marry again.

SECTION II.

Parties authorized to grant Permits of Marriage. 1.—All religious societies or churches of the freedmen or of other persons, whose organizations are recognized by their respective denominations, are authorized to grant permits for marriage, provided:

First. That the parties are of lawful age, and that neither have never been married.

Second. That if either or both have been married, that such party has complied with the conditions of Sec. I., Rules 2 and 3.

2.—Any society or church, having an ordained pastor, may delegate to him its power to examine applicants and grant permits for marriage. Such power, however, may be revoked at any time.

EARLY BLACK SOCIAL ORGANIZATIONS

BROTHER PRINCE HALL
WARRANTEE WORSHIPFUL MASTER. AFRICAN LODGE 459 A. L. 5784. A. D. 1784
FOUNDER OF COLORED FRATERNITY OF FREE AND ACCEPTED MASONS.
BOSTON, MASS.

Prince Hall

Born a slave in Massachusetts, **PRINCE HALL** (circa 1735-1807), a leather craftsmen and caterer, gained freedom through manumission from his owner shortly after the Boston Massacre in 1770. In 1775 Hall and 14 other black men were initiated into Freemasonry by a lodge attached to the British military stationed in Boston. Four months later, on July 3, they formed their own lodge, African Lodge No. 1.

Barred from (and not recognized by) local white lodges, the black Masons were issued a charter in 1787 as African Lodge No. 459 by the Grand Lodge of England, with Hall serving as its grand master. The organization actively denounced the slave trade, supported the efforts of fugitive slaves, and campaigned for schools for black children.

In a 1797 speech Hall spoke out against the hypocrisy and cowardliness of mob violence against blacks: "Patience, I say; for were we not possessed of a great measure of it, we could not bear up under the daily insults we meet with in the streets of Boston, much more on public days of recreation. How, at such times, are we shamefully abused, and that to such a degree, that we may truly be said to carry our lives in our hands, and the arrows of death are flying about our heads ... tis not for want of courage in you, for they know that they dare not face you man for man, but in a mob, which we despise...."

The lodge honored Hall after his death in 1807 by changing its name to Prince Hall Grand Lodge. Hall's African Masonic Lodge became forerunner to several African-American fraternal organizations including the African Society (Boston and New York) and Free African Society (Philadelphia). Many black fraternal organizations were mutual aid societies, providing social, political, and financial support and insurance to members. Activists in the fight for equal rights, they campaigned against slavery and for educational and employment opportunities for free blacks.

After the Civil War, black fraternal organizations, along with black churches, championed the fight for black voting rights and worked against the tide of segregationist laws.

Above: **HEROES OF THE COLORED RACE, 1881**
Most prominently displayed on the poster are Blanche K. Bruce, Frederick Douglass, and Hiram Revels. Lithograph.

Opposite, bottom: **GRAND LODGE NO. 2, GREENVILLE, ILLINOIS, 1897**

Richard Allen

SACRED LEGACIES

ANNETTE GORDON-REED

In Thomas D. Morris's *Southern Slavery and the Law 1619-1860* there is a description of a judicially ordered partition of slaves after the death of their "owner," Robert McCausland of Louisiana. The image is straightforward and devastating. Morris writes, "The slaves were divided into two lots, and the heirs drew the lots from slips of paper marked Lot 1 and Lot 2." Morris then reproduces the names of the people who were placed in each respective group. The list clearly shows that families were separated—husbands and wives, a mother from her infant—all to satisfy the property interests of the white slave owners who had the power to (and did) treat black slaves as something on the order of cattle.

Whenever I read this passage I am struck by how this episode reveals the rock-hard essence of American slavery: one group of people under the whim and control of another. Families were torn apart—or lived with the constant threat of separation—not because of the vagaries of nature, primitive health care, or dangerous occupations, but in the ordinary course of a social, economic, and legal system that promoted these types of atrocities. Make no mistake; in a society that treated human beings as property, and that placed the right to private property at the apex of its values, enslaved people could have no sure expectation of maintaining even the deepest, most elemental of their human connections. To the dominant culture, absolutely nothing about black life was sacred.

And yet, I know many things were sacred to enslaved people. They were human beings, and the desire for personal integrity, the impulse to create and maintain a family life, to build and be a part of a community, and to express spirituality in some manner, were as present within the community of slaves as they have been in all human societies. Although the humanity of slaves is universal—it speaks to all who choose to recognize it—it draws me in in a very specific way. Because I am black, the connection I feel to American slaves is particular in that it is racial. I simply cannot read about slave children, or see photographs or depictions of them, without at some point thinking of my own daughter and son. This is not to suggest that white observers of that time could not make the same connection, think of their own children and feel empathy and outrage at the very idea of human beings in that condition. The big difference, of course, is that my family would actually have been eligible for slavery. A doll or cradle that belonged to a slave child could have been my own daughter's toy or cradle had she been born a mere 140 years ago, not even the beginning of a blink of the eye of history. If one adds the decades after the end of the Civil War, when blacks in the South continued to live lives nearly as blighted as those of slaves, all this was not so long ago.

Truthfully, it is more useful to think of the black experience in America as being along a continuum—from slavery to a gradual move toward citizenship that is still ongoing. Considering it that way, as long as blacks are on the American continent they will be bound to the memories of their forebears who endured the almost unendurable. The chain cannot be broken.

It is significant that it was *black* people who were treated with such inhumanity. For American slavery was racially based, and sought to stamp an entire race of people with the mark of inferiority. Slavery nurtured not just "unfreedom," it promoted and sustained a doctrine of white supremacy that has outlasted the peculiar institution itself. Slavery and racism were inextricably entwined. That is why it is so important for us today to understand that time and be aware of its influences as we struggle to "overcome."

But how do we do this? There has been some debate about the proper approach to depicting both the operation of and effect of slavery on black culture. In one corner are those who believe that the incessant focus on the power of white slave owners neglects the story of blacks' efforts to resist the terms of their captivity—through the less common venue of slave rebellions or the more common route of negotiating within the boundaries of their very limited power to seek the best life they could. In this view the agency of the enslaved must be recognized, lest whites and blacks of today remain seduced by the fantasy of total white omnipotence and total black impotence. There is a legitimate fear that traces of that particular construction of the master-slave relationship will influence attitudes about racial hierarchies today. Although it won't be said out loud (except by the most racist members of society), the quiet assumption will remain that whites are naturally in power and blacks are naturally out of it. Hasn't it been that way from the beginning?

On the other hand, how much "power" can be given to slaves before slavery comes to resemble just an extremely bad employment situation? Those who are skeptical of the desire to highlight the agency of slaves wonder whether the focus on the slaves' ability to in some ways transcend their circumstances, however uplifting the stories might be, tends to distort the picture. The argument is that this minimizes the evil of slavery and obscures the guilt of slave owners who, by the very nature of their society, had the power of life and death over the enslaved. That slaves managed to make the best of their circumstances is a sidelight to the main point: They were the victims of naked aggression.

Which view is right? Perhaps the unsatisfactory answer is that they are both right. The better course of action, then, is to try to see slavery in all its aspects. There is simply no way for one book, one view, any one perspective to capture the experiences of a culture that spread itself out over three centuries. We should be sophisticated enough to see that. Slave agency and white power were not mutually exclusive phenomena. They both existed, and it is necessary to write clearly about both in as truthful a manner as possible. That is why the burgeoning interest in slavery expressed in books, movies, art and museum exhibits, and finally politics and law (with the rise of the reparations movement) is so important.

My own journey into thinking, learning, writing, and teaching about slavery and how it affects us today puts me more in the corner of those who are interested in how blacks survived under slavery. It is imperative to keep in mind that although white slave owners did have overwhelming power, they were not gods. That nothing of black life was sacred to whites did not mean that there was nothing sacred to black life. The inner lives of slaves could never have been the total province of the masters. Nothing shows that more clearly than the slaves' construction of their religious lives and their family lives.

As James Baldwin correctly observed, blacks transformed Christianity in America, unleashing it from its more "God-centered" moorings and turning it toward the ideal of Jesus, the Savior. The poetry of the Negro spirituals is a testament to that transformation, as the story of suffering and redemption in the Holy Land was transported to the fields of Georgia and Texas. Whatever message the masters were taking from the Bible, it is clear that the slaves were taking another. The substance of the holy text was not the only important lesson learned, however. The creation of a congregation, the establishment of leadership in the form of the preacher of the Gospel, showed black slaves that they were capable of organizing themselves as a community to achieve a stated goal—again, the link between the past, present, and future. Lessons learned, values adopted were carried from the slave quarter into the new world of freedom and beyond. Even today, some argue that the church remains the preeminent institution within the black community.

The same could be said of family life. That the law provided nothing in the way of protection for slave families did not prevent the notion of family from growing and remaining within the slave community. One of the most ironic aspects of the modern view of slavery is that some black Americans have been made to feel ashamed of their ancestors' condition, when it is so clear that it is not black people who have anything to be ashamed of. They did the best they could with what they had.

Family connections were maintained and strengthened through naming practices. Mothers, fathers, aunts, uncles, and cousins, who may have been separated by great distances, were kept a part of the fold by giving children their names. The practice of taking care of those who were not relatives took hold in slavery as well, forging a broader conception of family that was as much about duty and empathy as blood. This is the genius of adaptation.

Several years ago I attended a presentation given by Cinder Stanton and Dianne Swanne Wright at the International Center for Jefferson Studies. It was part of their Getting Word Project, which involves interviewing the descendants of people who were enslaved at Monticello. It is a marvelous effort that is yielding much vital information about the family and social life of slaves and free blacks. Stanton and Wright had put together a slide presentation that contained photographs of family members, some from the late 1840s and 1850s, up until the present.

As I sat in the dark listening to their words and studying the slides as they flashed across the screen, there was one moment that brought me near tears. It was the photo of a man named Peter Fossett, whose family had been scattered to the winds upon Thomas Jefferson's death in bankruptcy. Some members of the Fossett family, who later gained their freedom, worked hard and, with the help of friends, bought Peter Fossett's freedom. He moved to Ohio and became a prosperous caterer and a pillar of his church. There he was, dressed in his finest suit, looking as dignified as anyone who ever lived—and he was. It was awesome to think that this man started life as a chattel—an item of property—as did the rest of his family. Yet his face and demeanor told a different story. He was never just that. This was a human being. After his emancipation Fossett and his family, as did millions of other blacks, picked up their lives and went forward, taking with them the lessons of family loyalty, the importance of self-improvement, and faith. There is no better lesson that we can learn from the lives of the enslaved. If we want to be worthy of them, we must learn it.

Opposite:
GEORGE LYONS'S FAMILY TREE, 1783-1851
Family tree of George Lyons, grandfather of Maritcha Lyons.

Following pages:
FREE MEN IN RICHMOND, VIRGINIA, 1863

3

George Lyons 2nd

George Lyons 2nd was born in the year 1783 on Long Island.

Lucinda Lewis his wife was born in the year 1790 in Dutchess County, New York

George Lyons and Lucinda Lewis were married in Dutchess County, in the year 1807 and had eleven children.

Births.

Matilda, first child was born in Pesquage, Dutchess County, New York on the 5th day of March 1808.

Lyman, second child was born in Pesquage, Dutchess County, New York, January 1st 1810.

[Third child was born in Pl...]

George Lyons 2nd (continued) 5

Dutchess County, New York December 22nd 1812.

Albro, fourth child was born in Fishkill, Dutchess County, New York, February 10th 1814.

George, fifth child was born in Fishkill, Dutchess County, New York, March 14-1816.

Eliza Ann, sixth child was born in Jacob Street, New York City, September 18th 1818.

Colden, seventh child was born in Ferry Street, New York City, August 13th 1820.

Caroline, eighth child was born in Frankfort Street, New York City, March 1st 1823.

Hiram, ninth child was born in Gold Street, New York City, April 16th 1826.

Henrietta, tenth child was born in Amity Street (now West 3rd) New York City, May 20th 1830.

George Lyons 2nd (continued) 7

Theodore, eleventh child was born in Laurens Street (South 5th Ave - 1894. Now West Broadway - 1901) New York City, December 10th 1832.

In the year 1851, the following were all living and married viz;
Lyman in Pittsburg, Penn.
Albro in New York City.
George and wife in California.
Hiram in Brooklyn, N.Y.
Henrietta in Cincinatti, Ohio.

Marriages.

Matilda was married to Chas. Potter in New York City 1827,
Lyman was married to Eliza Allen of Fishkill, N.Y. in the city of New York in the year _____,

---

George Lyons 2nd (continued) 9

Deaths

Matilda, wife of Chas. Potter died September 22nd 1828. Age 20 years, 6 months, 17 days. No children. Was buried in St. Philips Cemetery, Christie Street, New York City.

Eliza Ann died August 26th 1819. Age 11 months, 6 days. Was buried in St. Philips Cemetery, Christie Street, New York City.

Caroline died December 12th 1823. Age 9 months, 11 days. Was buried in St. Philips Cemetery, New York City.

Theodore died July 11th 1835. Age 2 years, 7 months, 1 day. Was buried in Zion's Church burial ground, 85th Street, between 7th and 8th Aves, New York City,

Colden died October 16th 1838. Age 19 years, 2 months, 3 days. Buried

CHAPTER 6

A GLORY OVER EVERYTHING

The enslaved Africans who survived the Middle Passage and settled in the Americas came from diverse religious backgrounds. Though these religions numbered in the thousands, they frequently shared a number of common ideas about the nature of God and the universe and their relationships to the temporal and spiritual worlds. Most believed in an all-powerful God, the Supreme Being to whom they could speak directly through prayers, sacrifices, rituals, songs, and dances. A number of lesser gods who populated their spiritual and material universes could be called upon to address more mundane, day-to-day issues. Ancestors formed a part of their spiritual worlds, and they too could be summoned through prayers, rituals, and sacrifices to intervene on their behalf. The oldest living patriarch of the family or clan served as the priest of many of these religions. He was empowered to conduct ceremonies of worship and to preside over spiritual life of temples of worship and the family grounds. Spirits also dwelt on the land, in the trees, and on the rocks of the kinship group community as well as in the sky above and the waters that flowed through. God and the spirits were everywhere, and religion was so pervasive in traditional African life that it was present in all aspects of social, cultural, and political life. Religion was not simply a part of life, religion was life—so much so that there generally was no distinction in traditional African life between the sacred and the secular.

Rituals of worship included prayers and songs of adoration; the pouring of libations; and the sacrifice of chickens, sheep, goats, and, in some traditions, humans. Although human sacrifice was not widely practiced, prisoners and captives were offered in some areas to appease the gods. Much of the widely acclaimed African art includes ritual objects for various worship ceremonies. Singing, drumming, and the playing of a variety of musical instruments accompanied the individual and group dancing that was a common feature of traditional African religious practice.

Islam, which crossed from Arabia into Egypt in the seventh century, swept North Africa and the Iberian Peninsula. Below the Sahara, however, conversion was slow. Nevertheless, Islam became a religious alternative for

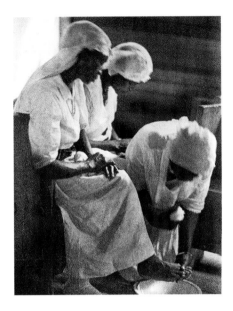

Above:
"WASHING THE SOULS OF THE FEET"
Photogravure, Doris Ulmann.

Opposite:
"ROLL, JORDAN, ROLL"
Photogravure, Doris Ulmann.

Africans in the kingdoms of Ghana, Mali, and Songhay as well as a number of other West African societies. Practitioners of Islam were among the African captives, and Islam became a New World African religious practice among enslaved Africans. One of the founding Christian churches was established in Ethiopia in the fourth century. Christianity also developed early on in North Africa. Not until the Portuguese missions arrived in the 16th century did Christianity even appear in West Africa, where the bulk of enslaved Africans were secured. A notable exception was the Kingdom of the Kongo where the king, and later his kingdom, converted to Christianity. The vast majority of African captives who were transported to the Americas had their first sustained encounter with Christianity in the Americas.

Most enslaved Africans were not able to keep up their traditional African religious practices in the Americas. Coming as they did from diverse religious backgrounds, they were obliged to invent something new in the Western Hemisphere. In the Caribbean and Central and South America, they invented New World African religions—syntheses of their diverse African religious practices or syntheses of African and Christian—usually Catholic—forms of worship. These included Candomblé and Umbanda in Brazil; Vodou in Haiti, Louisiana, and other Francophone communities; Santería in Cuba and Puerto Rico; and Shango in Trinidad and Grenada. Enslaved Africans used many of their traditional African rituals, ceremonies, songs, dances, and prayers to reinvent and adapt their African religious heritages to their New World realities. Drumming, dancing, the pouring of libations, animal sacrifice, and a firm belief in the existence, centrality, and omnipresent nature of God and the spirit world all survived the crossing of the Atlantic, but were expressed in new transformed African ways in the Americas.

In the United States, enslaved Africans transformed themselves in even more radical ways. During the colonial period, their religious practices likely mirrored those of enslaved Africans in other parts of the hemisphere. There is clear evidence that they frequently reassembled themselves along ethnic and national lines and tried to reproduce their traditional African rituals. Faced with the presence of other African ethnicities and nationalities, they frequently joined forces, like their counterparts in other parts of the hemisphere, to create new Pan-African rituals and ceremonies. Whereas most of Latin America and the Caribbean were Catholic religious environments,

THE GREAT AWAKENING

The religiously inspired Great Awakening that swept through the American colonies before the Revolutionary War brought many blacks into Christian conversion, particularly in northern Episcopal, Presbyterian, Methodist, and Congregational churches. White evangelical ministers who toured the country preaching a gospel of "salvation to all," regardless of race or economic status, were often perplexed but pleased to see generally uneducated blacks responding to their fiery messages in ways more biblical than those of whites—including ecstatic acts such as shouting, dancing, visions, trances, and "fits." Southern churches and slave owners were much less inclined to encourage or accept blacks. Slave owners commonly either regarded slaves as not intelligent enough to understand Christian principles or feared its doctrines of justice and injustice would lead to slave rebellions. African spiritual practices and Islamic beliefs were condemned as witchcraft.

In his autobiography, **From Slave Cabin to the Pulpit,** Peter Randolph recalled the secrecy and dangers involved in conducting camp meetings in Prince George County, Virginia: "Not being allowed to hold meetings on the plantation, the slaves assemble in the swamps, out of reach of the patrols. They have an understanding among themselves as to the time and place of getting together. This is often done by the first one arriving breaking boughs from the trees, and bending them in the direction of the selected spot."

African Americans remodeled Christianity's content and structure for their own cultural and spiritual needs. Services often took place in a slave cabin, field, or forest. Virtually all black churches were angered and indignant when white Christians used Scripture to defend slavery. In white southern churches selected Christian values were taught, including submissiveness and obedience. The central message to slaves was "Servants, obey your masters."

Coffin Point Praise House, St. Helena Island, South Carolina, circa 1900

135

The African Church, Richmond, Va.

THE RISE OF THE BLACK CHURCH

Secret or "invisible" churches were the first established by African Americans, free and enslaved. In rural regions of the South, clandestine churches were created to avoid detection by whites. The first "visible" church was founded in Silver Bluff, South Carolina, in 1750 by a plantation owner who allowed his slaves to worship. The first documented black minister for the Silver Bluff Baptist Church was George Liele (1752-1820), a licensed black clergyman from Georgia who preached in slave quarters along the Savannah River. In 1788 Andrew Bryan (1737-1812), who was converted by Liele, formally organized the **FIRST AFRICAN BAPTIST CHURCH OF SAVANNAH** (opposite, top).

THE FIRST AFRICAN BAPTIST CHURCH OF RICHMOND (above) traces its origins to 1780, when it had a mixed congregation of whites, "free colored," and slaves. In 1841 the white members sold the church to its 1,708 black members. The church installed its first black pastor in 1867.

In 1787 Richard Allen and Absalom Jones were among a group of blacks who sat in a pew reserved for whites at St. George's Methodist Episcopal Church in Philadelphia. Allen and Jones were infuriated when white ushers attempted to pull them from their seats during prayer. Both left with others to help found the Free African Society, a benevolent organization that became a model for other African societies nationwide.

In 1794 Jones and several other black members transformed the society into the **SAINT THOMAS AFRICAN EPISCOPAL CHURCH** (below). Rejecting Methodism altogether, Jones was made founding pastor. However, Allen, who wished to keep his Methodist connection, the same year founded another church—the Bethel African Methodist Episcopal Church—later the "mother" church of the A.M.E. denomination. In New York City **ST. PHILIP'S EPISCOPAL CHURCH** was an outgrowth of the rich and powerful Trinity Episcopal Church in Manhattan. Since the early 18th century blacks had worshiped at Trinity, primarily as slaves accompanying their owners. Segregated seating and separate services prompted Trinity's black congregants to form their own church. Blacks withdrew from Trinity in 1809 and were accepted into the Episcopal Diocese of New York in 1818 as the St. Philip's Colored Episcopal Church.

A Sunday Morning View of the African Episcopal Church of St. Thomas in Philadelphia.— Taken in June 1829.

JAMES VARICK

Born the son of a free father and a slave mother (who was manumitted when he was a small boy), Varick (1750-1827) was raised in Orange County, New York. When he was 16 he moved to New York City and joined the John Street Methodist Church. Trained as a shoemaker and licensed to preach, Varick left John Street in 1796 with a group of black church members and founded Zion Church, later known as Mother A.M.E. Zion. Varick became the first bishop of the African Methodist Episcopal Zion Church denomination.

the United States was overwhelmingly Protestant. The missionary activities of the two faces of Christendom in the Americas produced radically different results. In Latin America and the Caribbean, where Africans constituted the overwhelming majority of the population, Catholicism was never strong enough to displace the proto-traditional African religions. In the United States, on the other hand, where whites constituted the majority of the population, Christianity was more appealing to enslaved Africans. The Society for the Propagation of the Gospel in Foreign Parts, the missionary arm of the Church of England, tried to convert enslaved Africans in the United States to Christianity beginning in the 18th century. Allies of the slaveholders in their attempts to "civilize the heathen" Africans and make them better, more loyal servants, these early missionaries tried to teach the enslaved that they were born to be slaves, that they should work and serve their masters faithfully, and that they should never disobey their masters or lie or steal.

Most enslaved Africans were not deluded by such teachings, and these first efforts at Christianizing Africans in the United States failed miserably. It was perhaps the forms of worship practiced by the Baptists and the Methodists that resonated with the religious heritages of the enslaved Africans. Whereas the Roman Catholic liturgy and hierarchy created a distance between God, the spirit world, and religious congregants of this world, Protestant religions, especially the Baptist, accommodated many of the African traditions and practices. Initially, their message did not differ radically from that of the Episcopalians. But the Baptists and Methodists began to use slave and free black preachers as part of their proselytizing effort. These black preachers learned to read the Bible themselves and found within it liberating, life-affirming passages that refuted the teachings of white Christianity. In addition to serving at official church services, which were presided over and frequently monitored by whites, these preachers presided over frequent praise meetings, where they preached this liberating gospel. Within the confines of the slave quarters or in praise houses away from the farm or the plantation, enslaved Africans invented their own new Afro-Christian religious practices. Fusing remnants of their traditional African worship traditions with their own interpretations of the Christian faith, these praise meetings became unique New World African religious experiences. African-American oratory, music, and religious and theological worldviews are all rooted in the African Christian religious experience invented by enslaved Africans during the era of slavery.

Adorned grave site of Hackless Jenkins

AFRICAN BURIAL GROUNDS

The African Burial Ground

Cemeteries and burials were very special to free and enslaved African Americans. Even into the 20th century, burial insurance was often considered more important than life or accident insurance. Throughout the South graves were decorated or adorned in African-style traditions. Pottery or glass containers, including dishes, bowls, cups, shells, and clocks—sometimes set to mark the time of death—were commonly placed on graves. The purpose of the adornments was considered transitional (to ease the deceased into the spirit world) or to pacify the possible anger of the deceased. Some mourners considered it helpful to bury the personal items of the dead with them, so they would not come back to get them.

More than 10,000 enslaved African men, women, and children were buried at the **AFRICAN BURIAL GROUND** (left) in lower Manhattan. Unearthed during construction of a federal office building in 1991, the cemetery, which was in use from circa 1690 to 1795, covered more than five acres or about five city blocks. Eighteenth-century New York slavery laws forbade elaborate funeral processions and nighttime burials (the customary time for African funerary rituals), and no more than 12 mourners were permitted to attend an interment.

THE RELIGION OF THE SLAVE

GAYRAUD S. WILMORE

The traditional religions of Africa have a single overarching characteristic that survived for generations—a powerful belief that the individual and the community were continuously involved with the spirit world in the practical affairs of daily life. What many Europeans and Americans once regarded as a lower form of animism and pagan superstition in Africa is now recognized as highly involved ontological and ethical systems. This is partly because African scholars began to examine their own religions without the deferential accession to imported norms and values. On their part, African-American scholars have become more appreciative of their own African past and now generally hold that the slaves who were imported to the New World were not completely divested of their belief systems. Whatever was their precise nature, it is certain that those beliefs were not as unenlightened and preposterous as we once believed.

African religions know nothing of a rigid demarcation between the natural and the supernatural. All of life is permeated with forces or powers in some relationship to human weal or woe. Individuals are required, for their own sake and that of the community, to affirm this world of spirit, which merges imperceptibly with the immediate, tangible environment. One enters into communion with this other reality in a prescribed way to receive its benefits and avoid its penalties. The Supreme Being, ancestors, spirits resident in or associated with certain natural phenomena, and living humans who possess gifts of healing or of making mischief were all united in one comprehensive, invisible system, which has its own laws that sustain the visible world and ordinary life for the good of all.

Considerable injustice was done to the true nature of these beliefs by the early missionaries and others who could regard them only as "ignorant superstitions" or "dark and cruel fetishism." Even Du Bois, commenting upon *obi* or obeah worship, which he attributed to slaves who were transported to the West Indies, uncritically identified this form of religion with nature worship and witchcraft. What is suggested thereby is that we are dealing here with a perversion of the natural revelation of God, the weird concoction of a race of religious fanatics and charlatans. A somewhat more sophisticated analysis assumed that these religions were basically animistic and should be understood primarily as sorcery and magic. But such terms are pejorative, and the implication, when applied to the seminal religion of the slaves, is that they were ignorant and uncivilized persons; that to the degree that some vestige of the old beliefs survived, it must be responsible for the hysteria, degradation, and destructiveness of black religion.

African scholars have thrown a different light on these ancient structures of belief and practice and, therefore, on what may have been the true meaning of the religious background the slaves brought to the New World. Although many questions are still unanswered, it is possible to correct some popular presuppositions about the barbarity (as compared, let us say, with Christianity's part in the extermination of the American Indians) and inferiority of what the adherents of the traditional religions believed in the past and continue to believe today.

Formerly, the major emphasis was on the assumption of a strong predisposition for animism and nature worship. It is interesting to note that when American and European anthropologists did not understand what they were observing in a primal religion, the term "animism" usually cropped up. In the case of Africa it implied that the people found their gods in the sun, moon, stones, rivers, and in countless other natural objects or phenomena that had been desacralized in the West for a long time. The missionaries, in both America and Africa, assumed that this was an idolatrous practice having no soteriological or ethical meaning that could be related to the religion of Jesus.

Protestants, perhaps more than Catholics, were horrified by the native religions reported by travelers to West Africa. By the 17th and 18th centuries the Reformation was still a relatively recent occurrence, and Protestantism, especially the churches strongly influenced by Puritanism, was still reacting to what it considered the idolatry and paganism of Roman Catholicism.

Both Iberian Catholicism and Islam were less intolerant of the religious practices of Africans. But most Protestant missionaries saw little in them that represented "a preparation for the gospel." The use of charms, magic, ghosts, and witches was deplored as satanism. No religion that was essentially polytheistic, that countenanced polygamy, that made so much of ancestors, spirits, and the phenomena of nature, could provide an acceptable ground for Christianization. It first had to be stamped out to make way for the Gospel.

But the religions of Africa, for all their exotic peculiarities and strangeness to the European mind, were by no means crude and unenlightened. John S. Mbiti and others have shown that the widespread belief that the Africans worshiped nature and venerated animals as gods is a gross misunderstanding. Although the heavenly bodies and some animals often have a place in African religions, they are only two of several categories of being. They are symbolic representations of the living, pulsating environment in which humans subsist and through which we are related to the spirits of natural things and the ancestors, but preeminently to a Supreme Being, the God who is above all gods and who is known as Creator, Judge, and Redeemer.

Concerning this "nature worship" Mbiti has this to say about the central place of the sun in the religions of such peoples as the Ashanti and Igbo, two West African groups from which a considerable number of slaves were brought to the Americas: "Among many societies, the sun is considered to be a manifestation of God Himself.... There is concrete indication that the sun is considered to be God, or God considered to be the sun, however closely these may be associated. At best, the sun symbolizes aspects of God, such as His omniscience, His power, His everlasting endurance, and even His nature."

By far the most familiar criticism one hears of African religions is what Westerners regard as the inordinate reliance upon "medicine men," "conjurers," and other practitioners who are thought to dabble in magic or possess supernatural powers. Popular opinion has made such specialists little more than religious impostors and racketeers who make their living off the fears and gullibilities of primitive persons. As we have seen from Herskovits, not a few of them may have been among the shipments of slaves from

Dahomey and Togo, and it is they who may have formed the original cadres out of which the earliest black preachers began to emerge before they were recognized and instructed by whites. This partially explains the low estate in which most black preachers were held by the colonists before they became dependable representatives of the status quo.

It is true that all kinds of religious specialists must have been included among the slaves—from high priests and priestesses to village diviners and root doctors. It is necessary, however, to differentiate between the various roles those persons played and evaluate the contribution each made to the survival of the slave community. It is important to note, for example, that it is not certain that "conjurer" and "medicine man" are terms that can be employed indiscriminately to comprehend both good and bad magic. The term "medicine man" should be reserved for what we would call good magic. The conjurer, or witch doctor, plied his trade more frequently for antisocial purposes and was the object of fear among most African peoples. Such persons were sought out by those who wished to harm or destroy others. And because it was possible for bad magic to be turned back against the one who desired to use it for his or her own purposes, the conjurer was hated as well as feared. This was the person often blamed for whatever went amiss in the natural course of events and in the tempestuous interpersonal relationships under the conditions of slavery. In Africa a witch or conjurer was sometimes driven from the village, if not hunted down and slain.

On the other hand, the medicine man in African societies was a source of help and healing for the community in which he lived. Mbiti speaks of him as "the greatest gift" to the community and as "both doctor and pastor." He not only made use of plants, herbs, and minerals in his healing art, but was called upon for other ministrations. He gave such advice and counsel as persons needed to make themselves more productive and effective in the various departments of daily life—whether as warriors, farmers, husbands, or wives. He was, in other words, the precursor of the first "exhorters," "householders," or slave preachers who, with and without certification by white churches, became the religious leaders of the black community. Mbiti gives a summary description of this religious specialist in Africa: "In short, the medicine-men symbolize the hopes of society; hopes of good health, protection and security from evil forces, prosperity and good fortune, and ritual cleansing when harm or impurities have been contracted. These men and women are not fools; they are, on the average, intelligent and devoted to their work, and those who are not simply do not prosper or get too far."

This is, of course, a description of medicine men in contemporary Africa, but it is a considerably more dependable picture than the one we have from popular prejudice. This is not to deny that there were slaves who were the operators of a fraudulent mumbo-jumbo and who made a good living from the fear and credulity of their neighbors. Any inspection of the classified section of the *New York Amsterdam News*, the *Chicago Defender*, and other black newspapers across the country will attest to the fact that this kind of business is still carried on among certain segments of the black community. But most of the so-called conjure-men and "voodoo doctors" who rose to prominence in the secret meetings of the slaves were men of ability and integrity who took their vocations with the utmost seriousness. They were leaders who, in Mbiti's terms, symbolized the hopes of the community, who came to be called "Reverend," and were sought out for spiritual counsel and healing by both blacks and whites.

Originally, the prophets and preachers who evolved out of the African medicine men among the slaves attempted to direct the propitious, health-giving forces of nature to those who, despite the devastation of their ancestral culture, still believed in the efficacy of the spirit world and the protection of the gods and the spirits of the departed. They sold amulets, charms, "gre-gre bags" or hands (small parcels containing bits of paper, bones, or potions that were hung around the neck for protection and good luck). But their services were by no means confined to the use of magic. They also interpreted the meaning of events and called the people to a sense of solidarity, pride, and the first stirrings of resentment against their oppressors. Returning once more to Herskovits's theory that a specific group of priests were among the slaves brought from Dahomey, we cite again his argument about their role:

"It is apparent that here is a mechanism which may well account for the tenaciousness of African religious beliefs in the New World, which … bulk largest among the various elements of West African culture surviving. What could have more effectively aided in this than the presence of a considerable number of specialists who could interpret the universe in terms of aboriginal belief? What, indeed, could have more adequately sanctioned resistance to slavery than the presence of priests who, able to assure supernatural support to leaders and followers alike, helped them fight by giving the conviction that the powers of their ancestors were aiding them in their struggle for freedom?"

The early spiritual leaders among the slaves in the Caribbean and North American colonies were the representatives of the traditional religions of Africa that we are beginning to understand and appreciate today. What they brought to Christianity were attitudes and perspectives both in agreement and at variance with missionary teaching. For all of what has seemed to Westerners to have been weird and outlandish practices, these men and women retained an instinctive intelligence about existence, physical and mental health, and the presence in life of that which is radically antagonistic to and irreconcilable with the best interests of the community. They had a concept of a Supreme Being who was involved in the practical affairs of life, but in a different way than the Judeo-Christian God. This being was approachable through many intermediaries, but was known by various names, including Father and Mother, and whose power was supreme over all other powers of the universe. It was not only in the identification of the healing properties of plants and minerals, or in the exorcism of demonic influences, that these medicine men-preachers contributed to the security of the uprooted slave. What became most significant for a later period was the fact that they recognized the relationship between "bad magic" as whites practiced it and the dehumanizing situation in which they and their people found themselves.

It was from within an African religious framework that the slave made adjustments to Christianity after hearing the Gospel. The influences of the African religious past extended into their new life, first in the Caribbean and later in the United States and, far from being completely obliterated, were reshaped by the circumstances of enslavement. Slavery only served to drive those influences from the past beneath the surface by force and terror. But instead of decaying there, the African elements were enhanced and strengthened in the subterranean vaults of the unconscious whence they arose—time and time again during moments of greatest adversity and repression—to subvert the attempt to make the slave an emasculated, depersonalized version of a white person.

Christianity alone, adulterated, otherworldly, and disengaged from its most authentic implications—as it was usually presented to the slaves—could not have provided the slaves with all the resources they needed for the kind of resistance they expressed. It had to be enriched with the volatile ingredients of the African religious past and, most important of all, with the human yearning for freedom that found a channel for expression in the early black churches of the South.

Joseph R. Washington, Jr., made a significant contribution in the 1960s to the discussion about black folk theology when he observed: "Born in slavery, weaned in segregation and reared in discrimination, the religion of the Negro folk was chosen to bear the roles of both protest and relief. Thus, the uniqueness of black religion is the racial bond which seeks to risk its life for the elusive but ultimate goal of freedom and equality by means of protest and action. It does so through the only avenues to which its members have always been permitted a measure of access, religious convocations in the fields or in houses of worship."

But this religion, as the commonsense orientation, sagacity, and lifestyle of the folk, went far beyond religious convocations in fields and churches. It permeated the wit and wisdom, the music and literature, the politics and prophecy of a wide spectrum of black life in the highly secularized urban areas of the North, as well as in the rural communities of the South. It was the soil out of which grew the syncretistic, militant black nationalism and the African culture interests of many cults in the ghettos of Harlem, Watts, Chicago, and other communities. It erupted intermittently, like an underwater volcano, in the music of Mahalia Jackson and Duke Ellington and in the writings of some who are otherwise as far apart as James Baldwin and Amiri Baraka. It inundated the black churches of the South and many in the North during the height of the civil rights movement when Dr. Martin Luther King, Jr., was its high priest and the Southern Christian Leadership Conference its institutional "church." Those strains of black religion that have been least influenced by white Christianity have played an important role in the quest for racial justice and are inseparable from black culture as a whole.

All of its deficiencies and excesses notwithstanding, the religion that the slaves practiced was their own. It was unmistakably the religion of an oppressed, but not entirely conquered, people. It had, of course, common features with Euro-American Protestantism and, in the French-speaking and Spanish-speaking Caribbean, with Roman Catholicism. But it was born out of the experience of being black and understanding blackness to be some- how connected with being held in bondage and needing to be free. Its most direct antecedents were the quasi-religious meetings that took place on the plantations, unimpeded by white supervision and under the leadership of the first generation of African priests who were to become preachers. It was soon suppressed and dominated by the religious instruction of the Society for the Propagation of the Gospel in Foreign Parts and the Baptist, Methodist, and Presbyterian churches. But the black faith that evolved from the coming together of diverse religious influences became a *tertium quid,* something distinctly different from any of its major contributors.

Both the slave congregations of the South—"the invisible institution"— and the more or less free black churches of the North developed a religion that masked a sublimated outrage balanced with patience, cheerfulness, and a boundless confidence in the ultimate justice of God. As the religion of a subjugated people, it had both positive and negative effects upon those who participated in it. It served, in formal and informal ways, to order and inter- pret an existence that was characterized on the one hand by repression, self- abnegation, and submissiveness, and on the other by subterfuge, opportunism, and the joyous affirmation of life despite tribulation.

BONDS UNLOOSED AND BROKEN

People in the African continent spoke thousands of languages during the slavery era. It should come as no surprise, then, that those African captives who were enslaved in the Americas also spoke a wide variety of languages upon their arrival in the Western Hemisphere. Sometimes two or more from the same ethnic or national group spoke the same language and so could communicate with one another. If they were to communicate with Africans from other cultural or linguistic families or with those who held them captive and controlled their lives, a new linguistic strategy was necessary. Over time, whenever enslaved Africans encountered this dilemma, they created vernacular Creole versions of their respective colonial languages. In the cauldron of slavery, African captives of diverse linguistic backgrounds created new languages to communicate with each other and with their respective enslavers. Wherever slavery existed they created these New World vernacular languages. Appropriating the vocabulary of the enslavers' language, they incorporated it into traditional African grammatical and linguistic structures and created new American languages by fusing and synthesizing African and European elements.

These vernacular Creole languages became the foundation of the languages African peoples speak throughout the Americas today. Neither "bad" versions of English, French, Dutch, Spanish, or Portuguese, nor reflections of blacks' intellectual or linguistic deficiencies, these New World African languages became the fundamental means of communication among the diverse African peoples of the Americas. They served the needs of their inventors and continue to inform the language patterns and cultural preferences of present-day practitioners. Ordinary day-to-day speech, as well as the songs, folk tales, and certain vernacular-based literatures of ordinary African peoples are spoken, written, and sung in these Creole languages. The presence of these African vernacular languages also transformed the European languages spoken by whites in the Americas. Southern American vernacular language, a product of the interaction of Africans and Europeans in the American South, has its counterparts in language spoken by whites throughout the hemisphere.

Fifteen Dollars Reward!
NOTICE

IS hereby given, that my Negro man named YETT won't stay at home, but runs at large, to and fro. All persons are therefore forbidden to harbor, trust or employ said run-away, even one hour, on penalty of the law; and no excuse will be taken of those who transgress this injunction.

YETT is pretty large sized; not of the blackest order; speaks Low-Dutch and broken English; and plays upon the *fiddle*.

The above reward will be paid to any person who will safely return said Negro into the custody of the subscriber, residing about two miles from *Ingham's Mills*.

Simon I. Toll.

Oppenheim, March 24, 1824.   c33t3

Above:

REWARD NOTICE FOR BILINGUAL RUNAWAY SLAVE, 1824

Oppenheim, New York.

The advertisement acknowledges Yett's bilingual capability, a quality shared by many enslaved Africans.

Opposite:

WHITE MAN READING TO A GROUP OF AFRICAN MEN AND BOYS, CIRCA 1890

Most slaves were illiterate, but a few liberal plantation owners gave their "property" a rudimentary education.

Preceding pages:

CHURCH PICNIC, CIRCA 1900

Black churches offered spiritual guidance and religious instruction, and were often the black community's primary center for political activity or social gatherings. In urban areas, many black churches provided social services such as food kitchens, educational tutoring, and employment information.

POLYGLOTTA AFRICANA, 1854

This comparative vocabulary of words and phrases in more than a hundred distinct African languages illustrates the linguistic diversity of continental Africans.

Some enslaved Africans and their descendants mastered the standard versions of colonial English, Spanish, French, Portuguese, and Dutch. Many became bilingual and trilingual, speaking two or more colonial or Native American languages. Runaway slave notices provide ample testimony of the linguistic proficiency of enslaved Africans. Learning to read and write in these languages posed new challenges for enslaved Africans and their descendants.

In traditional African societies cultural knowledge was recorded and passed on from generation to generation by priests, respected elders, griots, and storytellers. Except in certain Islamic communities and a very few traditional African ones, learning and socializing depended on the oral tradition rather than the study of books and written texts. Reading and writing were not central to the lives and experiences of the African communities from which the enslaved African population came. In the context of slavery, however, enslaved Africans were introduced to the forms of literacy—reading and writing—in the respective colonial languages that were central to the organization of European colonial societies. In the United States, whites were initially ambivalent about whether or not it was wise to teach blacks to read and write.

Encouraged by missionaries because they wanted to teach blacks to read the Bible, some slaveholders during the colonial era not only permitted but at times encouraged some Africans to learn to read and write. Others permitted their children to teach young black slave playmates to read. Still others encouraged intelligent young blacks to become literate because they could use these skills to handle their paperwork. Other slaveholders objected to such practices because they believed literacy and knowledge and slavery were incompatible. Knowledge, they believed, fueled the freedom impulse, which in turn led literate slaves to run away. The ability to write also made it possible for blacks to forge passes and otherwise subvert the systems of social control used to manage blacks.

The Nat Turner rebellion of 1831 led to a tightening of restrictions on slave literacy. Citizens of Southampton, Virginia, where the rebellion took place, passed a resolution claiming that the education of persons of color was "inexpedient and improper as it is calculated to cause them to be dissatisfied with their condition and furnishes the slave with the means of absconding from his master." Eventually, anti-literacy statutes became the norm in southern society.

Above: Freedmen's school, North Carolina Below: Zion School for Colored Children, 1866 Charleston, South Carolina.

FREEDMEN'S SCHOOLS

After the war, newly freed slaves clamored for education, as laws that barred slaves from learning to read and write had ended. Children, adults, and elderly blacks filled classrooms and schoolhouses, and where schools did not exist, they took their lessons in fields. Maj. Gen. Oliver Otis Howard (1830-1909), Commissioner of the Freedmen's Bureau, took an active interest in educating former slaves. Working with private donors, charities, and aid societies to build and support schools, the Bureau participated in the construction, furnishing, and upkeep of schools and the purchase of schoolbooks. Northern aid societies contributed to the development of schools for emancipated slaves, and the Bureau assisted their participation by acting as liaison for the freedmen. Organizations such as the American Tract Society and the Freedman's Union Commission also helped find teachers who were adequately trained. The greatest achievements of the Freedmen's Bureau were in education. More than a thousand black schools were built and nearly $500,000 spent to establish teacher-training organizations. All major black colleges were either founded by, or received aid from, the Bureau. In Washington, D.C., the Howard Normal and Theological Institute for Education of Teachers and Preachers (Howard University), named for General Howard, received its charter in 1867. In 1866 the Fisk School (Fisk University) in Nashville, Tennessee, was named for General Clinton B. Fisk (1828-1890) of the Tennessee Freedmen's Bureau.

FREEDOM'S JOURNAL.

"RIGHTEOUSNESS EXALTETH A NATION."

CORNISH & RUSSWURM,
Editors and Proprietors.

NEW-YORK, FRIDAY, JUNE 22, 1827.

VOL. I. NO. 15

From the Alexandria Gazette.
VIEWS
Of the Benevolent Society of Alexandria for ameliorating and improving the condition of

ly, he soon learns to consider every kind of labour as exceedingly irksome, and even degrading to the rank of a gentleman. The whole business of his life is to spend the fruits of others' labour: and if he be reduced

gained! For the first month, however, things went on tolerably smooth—a newly married husband will pardon much in a good-looking wife—even her tongue—the only edge-tool, I should add, which never wears out by constant

From what other source can the mind of man receive satisfaction on every point of duty and of hope? Where shall we look for a system of instruction that meets every exigency, and answers all the purposes of a reli

In the United States, they became sufficiently proficient that they wrote and published literary, theological, and artistic works in the standard idiom. Here, these enslaved Africans and former slaves—frequently fugitives—published books, personal narratives, poetry, fiction, essays, social commentary, and newspapers. Jupiter Hammon, slave-poet from New York, is generally credited with being the first published black author. Phillis Wheatley, a Senegalese-born African slave living in Massachusetts, published the first book of poems by an African in 1773. Other slaves and ex-slaves—Frederick Douglass, William Wells Brown, and Samuel Ringgold Ward—all distinguished themselves as writers.

During slavery, the dominant form of formal education available to enslaved Africans was apprenticeships. Selected individuals were apprenticed to master craftsmen to learn their crafts. In time, enslaved Africans or free blacks who had learned their crafts through the apprenticeship system provided a significant percentage of the skilled labor on plantations and in urban areas.

The first schools for blacks were established in Charleston, South Carolina (1695), and New York City (1704), respectively. The New York African Free School, founded by the New York Manumission Society in 1787, trained some of the principal black leaders of the 19th century. Lincoln University, the first historically black college in the United States, was founded in 1854, and Wilberforce University, which opened in 1856, was purchased by the A.M.E. Church in 1862, making it the first U.S. university controlled by African Americans. Within two decades of the end of the Civil War, a vast network of black colleges had been established by and for the first generation of free men and women. Howard University (1867), Atlanta University (1865), Meharry Medical College (1876), Hampton University (1868), Spelman College (1881), and Tuskegee Institute (1881), among others, all trace their roots to this period. Equally important, by 1870, over 20 percent of the newly freed blacks in the American South were literate.

Opposite top:
SMALL WOODEN SCHOOLHOUSE
African Americans sit outside a school in Savannah, Georgia, circa 1895.

Opposite bottom:
FREEDOM'S JOURNAL, 1827
In 1827 Samuel Cornish and John Russwurm founded the nation's first black newspaper, Freedom's Journal, *in New York City.*

POEMS

ON

VARIOUS SUBJECTS,

RELIGIOUS AND MORAL.

BY

PHILLIS WHEATLEY,

NEGRO SERVANT to Mr. JOHN WHEATLEY,
of BOSTON, in NEW ENGLAND.

L O N D O N:
Printed for A. BELL, Bookseller, Aldgate; and sold b
Messrs. COX and BERRY, King-Street, *BOSTON.*
M DCC LXXIII.

*Publiſhed according to Act of Parliament, Septr. 1. 1773 by Archd. Bell,
Bookſeller No. 8 near the Saracens Head Aldgate.*

PUBLISHED AFRICAN AMERICANS

PHILLIS WHEATLEY (circa 1753-1784) was the first African American to publish a book of poems and the first to garner national-al and international acclaim as a writer. As poetry was regarded as the highest level of human expression, and blacks were thought inca-pable of high artistic achievement, many did not believe Wheatley, an African-born slave, could have written such poetry. When **POEMS ON VARIOUS SUBJECTS, RELIGIOUS AND MORAL** by Phillis Wheatley, Negro Servant to Mr. John Wheatley of Boston, in New England, was published in the fall of 1773, no fewer than 18 of Boston's most distinguished gentlemen pledged to the authorship of her work. Many reviewers contended that her poems revealed her humanity and they further argued that anyone so capable of artistic expression should not be enslaved. Wheatley was granted her freedom soon after publication of her book. **OLAUDAH EQUIANO** (Gustavus Vassa 1750?-1797), the son of an East Nigerian chief, was kidnapped at the age of ten and taken to Virginia, where he was purchased by a lieutenant in the Royal Navy and transported to England. His owner named him for 16th-century Swedish king Gustavus Vasa. In 1761 Equiano was sold in the West Indies to a Philadelphia Quaker and merchant from whom he learned commercial arts. He traveled between Philadelphia and the West Indies, earning enough money by trading in the Caribbean to purchase his freedom in 1766. His acclaimed autobiography, **THE INTERESTING NARRATIVE OF OLAUDAH EQUINO**, had eight British editions and

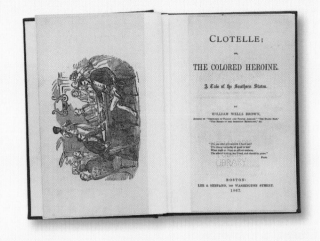

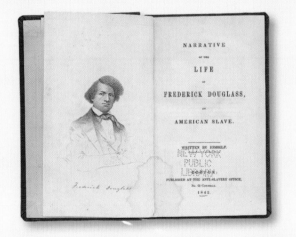

one American publication in his lifetime, and ten posthumously, including Dutch and German translations. **THE ANGLO-AFRICAN MAGAZINE, 1859,** was one of the earliest literary journals by African Americans. It was published by **THOMAS HAMILTON** and featured writing by J. W. C. Pennington, Sarah Douglas, Edward W. Blyden, William C. Nell, Daniel Payne, James McCune Smith, Frances Ellen Watkins, and Martin Delaney. It included history, biography, social criticism, poetry, reviews, essays, and short stories. **NARRATIVE OF THE LIFE OF FREDERICK DOUGLASS, AN AMERICAN SLAVE,** 1845. Douglass was born into slavery in Maryland in 1818. **FREDERICK DOUGLASS' PAPER,** October 2, 1851, Rochester, New York, began as the **NORTH STAR** in 1847 and became the **DOUGLASS MONTHLY** after 1860. **CLOTELLE; OR THE PRESIDENT'S DAUGHTER: A NARRATIVE OF SLAVE LIFE IN THE UNITED STATES** by **WILLIAM WELLS BROWN,** 1867. Born a slave on a Kentucky plantation, author and abolitionist William Wells Brown escaped to Canada in 1834, where he worked helping fugitive slaves cross Lake Erie by steamboat. Brown is considered the first African American to author works in several literary genres. His **CLOTELLE,** although fictional, was based on the 19th-century rumor that Thomas Jefferson had fathered slave children. His play **THE ESCAPE; OR, A LEAP FOR FREEDOM** became the first drama published by an African American.

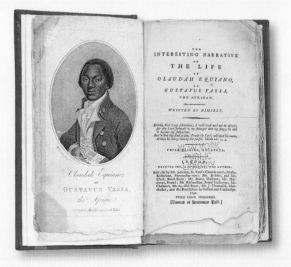

ONE-ROOM SCHOOL, HENDERSON COUNTY, KENTUCKY, CIRCA 1900S

Barefoot children work at their desks under the supervision of a single teacher, who taught all the ages and grades.

COLLEGES FOR AFRICAN AMERICANS

Booker T. Washington

Black churches were first to view education as the key to rising up the ladder of American society. Even during slavery, churches were the secret learning place for children and adults. In 1867 Augusta Institute (now **MOREHOUSE COLLEGE** in Atlanta) conducted its first classes in the basement of Springfield Baptist Church. In 1881 the Atlanta Baptist Female Seminary (**SPELMAN COLLEGE**) met in a church basement. On July 4, 1881, **BOOKER T. WASHINGTON** (1856-1915), hired as the school's first principal, opened the Tuskegee Normal School (**TUSKEGEE UNIVERSITY**, Alabama) in a shed next to a black church. Washington, who championed industrial education as the key to success for African Americans, required students to learn a trade and do manual labor at the school, including making and laying the bricks for campus buildings. Because Washington was principal (and white teachers either would not or were not expected to work beneath him) Tuskegee became the first black institution of advanced learning with a black faculty. His accommodationalist approach to race relations made him popular among white benefactors, gaining substantial funding and worldwide recognition for Tuskegee. In 1868 **BRIG. GEN. SAMUEL CHAPMAN ARMSTRONG** (1839-1893), who commanded the U.S. Ninth Colored Troops Regiment in the Civil War, founded a school for emancipated slaves in Hampton, Virginia. Acting on behalf of the Freedmen's Bureau, Armstrong espoused a philosophy of education, known as the Hampton Idea, that stressed the development of industrial skills, good moral character, and strong work ethic. In the early 20th century W. E. B. Du Bois criticized Hampton for its industrial curriculum.

Lincoln University, Southern Chester County, Pennsylvania

Above: Howard University, Washington, D.C.

Du Bois argued that African Americans needed to place greater emphasis on higher education to advance beyond manual labor jobs. **LINCOLN UNIVERSITY**, Southern Chester County, Pennsylvania, the oldest black institution of higher learning, was founded in 1854 by Presbyterian minister John Miller Dickey. Dickey's frustration with failing to secure admission for James Ralston Amos at Princeton University Seminary or at a Presbyterian religious academy led to the founding of an "institution for 'colored' men." Amos was the treasurer of the building fund for the national A.M.E. Church, which purchased **WILBERFORCE UNIVERSITY** (Ohio) in 1862 and merged it with A.M.E. Union Seminary a year later. The new Wilberforce thus became the first institution of higher learning founded by blacks.

Hampton University, Hampton, Virginia

THE TALKING BOOK

HENRY LOUIS GATES, JR.

[A] disingenuous and unmanly Position *had been formed; and privately* (and as it were in the dark) *handed to and again, which is this, that the* Negro's, *though in their Figure they carry some resemblances of Manhood, yet are indeed* no Men … *[The] consideration of the shape and figure of our* Negro's *Bodies, their Limbs and Members; their Voice and Countenance, in all things according with other Mens; together with their* Risibility *and* Discourse *(Man's peculiar Faculties) should be sufficient Conviction. How should they otherwise be capable of* Trades, *and other no less Manly imployments; as also of* Reading *and* Writing…*were they not truly Men?*

Morgan Godwyn, 1680

Let us to the Press Devoted Be,
Its Light *will* Shine *and* Speak Us Free.

David Ruggles, 1835

The literature of the slave, published in English between 1760 and 1865, is the most obvious site to excavate the origins of the Afro-American literary tradition. Whether our definition of tradition is based on the rather narrow lines of race or nationality of authors, upon shared themes and narrated stances, or upon repeated and revised tropes, it is to the literature of the black slave that we must turn to identify the beginning of the Afro-American literary tradition.

"The literature of the slave" is an ironic phrase, at the very least, and is an oxymoron at its most literal level of meaning. "Literature," as Samuel Johnson used the term, denoted an "acquaintance with 'letters' or books," according to the *Oxford English Dictionary*. It also connoted "polite or human learning" and "literary culture." While it is self-evident that the ex-slave who managed (as Frederick Douglass put it) to "steal" some learning from his or her master and the master's texts was bent on demonstrating to a skeptical public an acquaintance with letters or books, we cannot honestly conclude that slave literature was meant to exemplify either polite or humane learning or the presence in the author of literary culture. Indeed, it is more accurate to argue that the literature of the slave consisted of texts that represent impolite learning, and that these texts collectively railed against the arbitrary and inhumane learning that masters foisted upon slaves to reinforce a perverse fiction of the "natural" order of things.

The slave, by definition, possessed at most a liminal, or barely perceptible, status within the human community. To read and to write was to transgress this nebulous realm of liminality. The slave's texts, then, could not be taken as specimens of a black literary culture. Rather, the texts of the slave could only be read as testimony of defilement: the slave's representation and reversal of the master's attempt to transform a human being into a commodity, and the slave's simultaneous verbal witness of the possession of a humanity shared with Europeans. The slave wrote not primarily to demonstrate humane letters, but to demonstrate his or her own membership in the human community.

Black writers to a remarkable extent have created texts that express the broad "concord of sensibilities" shared by persons of African descent in the Western hemisphere. Texts written over two centuries ago address what we might think of as common subjects of condition that continue to be strangely resonant and relevant as we enter the 21st century. Just as there are remarkably few literary traditions whose first century's existence is determined by texts created by slaves, so too are there few traditions that claim such an apparent unity from a fundamental political condition represented for over two hundred years in such strikingly similar patterns and details. Has a common experience, or, more accurately, the shared sense of a common experience, been largely responsible for the sharing of what I like to think of as this text of blackness? It would be foolish to say no.

What seems clear upon reading the texts created by black writers in English or the critical texts that responded to these black writings is that the production of literature was taken to be the central arena in which persons of African descent could, or could not, establish and redefine their status within the human community. Black people, the evidence suggests, had to represent themselves as "speaking subjects" before they could even begin to destroy their status as objects, as commodities, within Western culture. In addition to all of the myriad reasons for which human beings write books, this particular reason seems to have been paramount for the black slave. At least since 1600 Europeans had wondered aloud whether or not the African "species of men," as they most commonly put it, could ever create formal literature, could ever master the arts and sciences. If they could, then, the argument ran, the African variety of humanity and the European variety were fundamentally related. If not, then it seemed clear that the African was destined by nature to be a slave.

Determined to discover the answer to this crucial quandary, several Europeans and Americans undertook experiments in which young African slaves were tutored and trained along with white children. Phillis Wheatley was merely one result of such an experiment. Francis Williams, a Jamaican who took the B.A. at Cambridge before 1750; Jacobus Capitein, who earned several degrees in Holland; Wilhelm Amo, who took the doctorate degree in philosophy at Halle; and Ignatius Sancho, who became a friend of Laurence Sterne and who published a volume of *Letters* in 1782, are just a few of the black subjects of such experiments. The published writings of these black men and one woman, who wrote in Latin, Dutch, German, and English, were seized upon both by pro- and anti-slavery proponents as proof that their arguments were sound.

So widespread was the debate over "the nature of the African" between 1730 and 1830 that not until the Harlem Renaissance would the work of black writers be as extensively reviewed as it was in the 18th century. Phillis Wheatley's list of reviewers includes Voltaire, Thomas Jefferson, George Washington, Samuel Rush, and James Beatty, to list only a few. Francis

Williams's work was analyzed by no less than David Hume and Immanuel Kant. Hegel, writing in the *Philosophy of History* in 1813, used the absence of writing by Africans as the sign of their innate inferiority. The list of commentators is extensive, amounting to a "who's who" of the French, English, and American Enlightenment.

Why was the creative writing of the African of such importance to the 18th century's debate over slavery? After Descartes, reason was privileged, or valorized, over all other human characteristics. Writing, especially after the printing press became so widespread, was taken to be the visible sign of reason. Blacks were reasonable, and hence "men," if—and only if—they demonstrated mastery of "the arts and sciences," the 18th century's formula for writing. So, while the Enlightenment is famous for establishing its existence upon man's ability to reason, it simultaneously used the absence and presence of reason to delimit and circumscribe the very humanity of the cultures and people of color which Europeans had been "discovering" since the Renaissance. The urge toward the systematization of all human knowledge, by which we characterize the Enlightenment, in other words led directly to the relegation of black people to a lower rung on the Great Chain of Being, an 18th-century metaphor that arranged all of creation on the vertical scale from animals and plants and insects through man to the angels and God himself.

By 1750 the chain had become individualized; the human scale rose from "the lowliest Hottentot" (black South Africans) to "glorious Milton and Newton." If blacks could write and publish imaginative literature, then they could, in effect, take a few giant steps up the Chain of Being. The Rev. James W. C. Pennington, an ex-slave who wrote a slave narrative and who was a prominent black abolitionist, summarized this curious idea in his prefatory note to Ann Plato's 1841 book of essays, biographies, and poems: "The history of the arts and sciences is the history of individuals, of individual nations." Only by publishing books such as Plato's, he argues, can blacks demonstrate "the fallacy of that stupid theory *that nature has done nothing but fit us for slaves, and that art cannot unfit us for slavery!*"

Not a lot changed, then, between Phillis Wheatley's 1773 publication of her *Poems* and Ann Plato's, except that by 1841 Plato's attestation was supplied by a black person. What we might think of as the black text's mode of being, however, remained pretty much the same during these 68 years. What remained consistent was that black people could become speaking subjects only by inscribing their voices in the written word. If this matter of recording an authentic black voice in the text of Western letters was of widespread concern in the 18th century, then how did it affect the production of black texts, if indeed it affected them at all? It is not enough simply to trace a line of shared argument as context to show that blacks regarded this matter as crucial to their tasks; rather, evidence for such a direct relationship of text to context must be found in the black texts themselves.

The most salient indication that this idea informed the writing of black texts is found in a topos, or repeated theme, that appears in five black texts published in English by 1815. This topos assumed such a central place in the black use of figurative language that we can call it a trope. It is the trope of the Talking Book, which first occurred in a 1770 slave narrative and was then revised in other slave narratives published in 1785, 1787, 1789, and 1815. This shared but revised trope argues forcefully that blacks were intent on placing their individual and collective voices in the text of Western letters, but also that even the earliest writers of the Anglo-African tradition read each other's texts and grounded these texts in what soon became a tradition. In the slave narratives discussed here, making the white written text speak with a black voice is the initial mode of inscription of the metaphor of the double-voiced.

The explication of the trope of the Talking Book reveals, rather surprisingly, that the curious tension between the black vernacular and the literate white text, between the spoken and written word, between the oral and the printed forms of literary discourse, has been represented and thematized in black letters at least since slaves and ex-slaves met the challenge of the Enlightenment to their humanity by literally writing themselves into being through carefully crafted representations in language of the black self.

Literacy, the very literacy of the printed book, stood as the ultimate parameter by which to measure the humanity of authors struggling to define an African self in Western letters. It was to establish a collective black voice through the sublime example of an individual text, and thereby to register a black presence in letters, that most clearly motivated black writers, from the Augustan Age to the Harlem Renaissance. Voice and presence, silence and absence, then, have been the resonating terms of a four-part homology in our literary tradition well over 200 years.

The trope of the Talking Book became the first repeated and revised trope of the tradition. The paradox of representing, of containing somehow, the oral within the written, precisely when oral black culture was transforming itself into a written culture, proved to be of sufficient concern for five of the earliest black autobiographers to repeat the same figure of the Talking Book that fails to speak, appropriating the figure accordingly with embellished rhetorical differences.

This general question of the voice in the text is compounded in any literature, such as the Afro-American literary tradition, in which the oral and the written literary traditions comprise separate and distinct discursive universes that, on occasion, overlap, but often do not. Precisely because successive Western cultures have privileged written art over oral or musical forms, the writing of black people in Western languages has, at all points, remained political, implicitly or explicitly, regardless of its intent or its subject. Then, too, since blacks began to publish books they have been engaged in one form of direct political dialogue or another, consistently up to the present. The very proliferation of black written voices, and the concomitant political import of them, led fairly rapidly in our literary history to demands both for the coming of a "black Shakespeare or Dante," as one critic put it in 1925, and for an authentic black printed voice of deliverance, whose presence would, by definition, put an end to all claims of the black person's subhumanity. In the black tradition, writing became the visible sign, the commodity of exchange, the text and technology of reason.

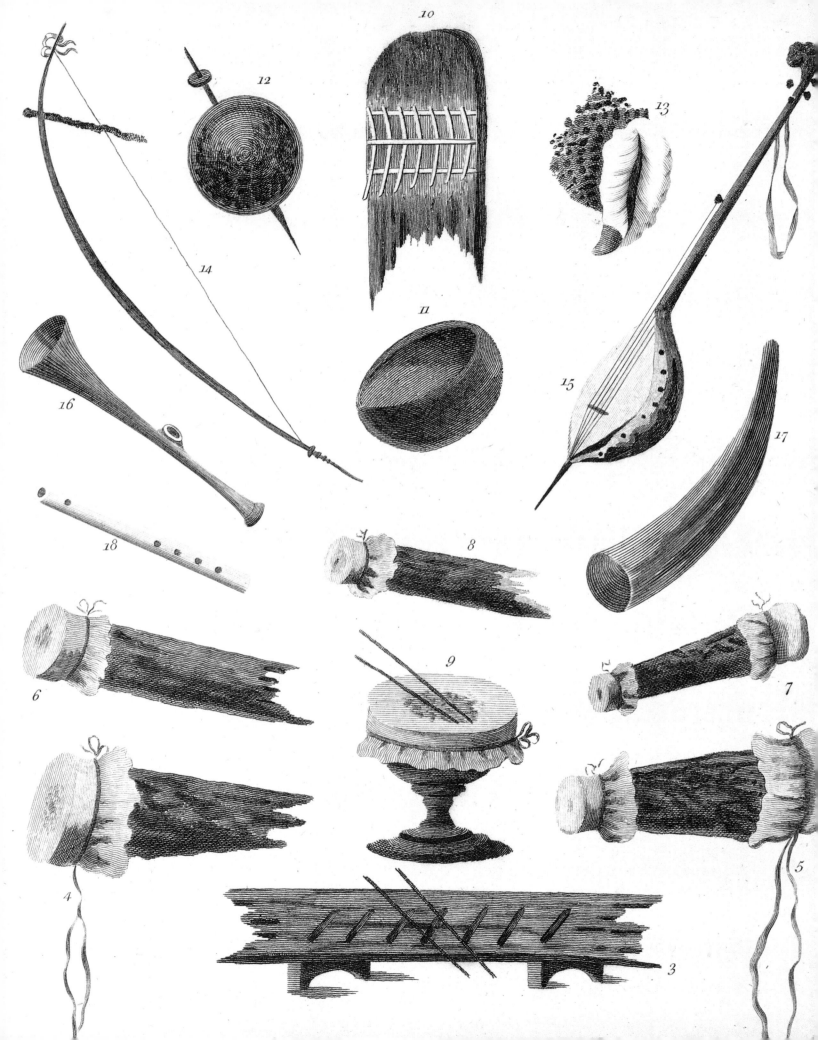

CHAPTER 8

THE SACRED FIRE

Most traditional West African societies, the sources of the vast majority of enslaved Africans in the Americas, had dynamic, vibrant, expressive cultures. The languages spoken were unusually animated, by most European standards. Peppered with proverbs, they were sources of moral and ethical training as well as simple vehicles of communication. Everyday conversation, as well as storytelling and oratory during sacred rituals and other performance events, was filled with energy and dynamism. Indigenous musics, which were extremely complex, permeated all aspects of traditional African social life. They were used to establish and maintain the rhythms of work. No festival or life-cycle celebration was complete without the presence of music, the moving rhythmic center of traditional African social and cultural life.

Dancing to these rhythms was equally pervasive. Such dancing challenged the rhythmic sensibilities of talented performers. Led by acrobatic leaders, who were frequently priests dressed in masks and elaborate costumes, communities of dancers frequently involved all members of society regardless of age, sex, or social status. When combined with the spiritual forces that frequently accompanied or were invoked by the singing, drumming, and dancing, the dancers themselves became the embodiment of the rhythms and the spirits. Whether in sacred religious ritual or day-to-day routines, music and the rhythms it evoked were constant, energizing, engrossing partners. And where music was heard, dancing was usually not far behind.

On board slave ships during the Middle Passage, enslaved Africans were frequently forced to dance. Once a day, some of them were brought up from the hold and encouraged to drum, sing, and dance. Slave captains believed that dancing enlivened the captives' spirits and reduced their sense of pain, suffering, and longing. Dancing was also seen as a form of exercise, which helped to preserve and maintain the captives' health during the tedious voyage. Ultimately, the slave captains were not really concerned about the health and well-being of their captives. Rather, they took whatever measures that were necessary to protect their human cargo to ensure that they would get a good return on their investments when the slaves were sold in the Americas.

Above:

ENSLAVED AFRICANS DANCING, CIRCA 1840

As an aid to good health, slaves were periodically taken on deck for exercise and fresh air. While they were being "danced" on deck, the crew cleaned and disinfected their quarters with vinegar.

Opposite:

MUSICAL INSTRUMENTS OF THE AFRICAN NEGROES, 1796

Etching by William Blake. Illustration from Narrative of a Five Years' Expedition Against the Revolted Negroes of Surinam by Captain John G. Stedman

Preceding pages:

TUSKEGEE HISTORY CLASS, 1902

Tuskegee's founder, Booker T. Washington, taught that blacks should strive first for economic self-improvement, and gains in civil rights would follow. However, W.E.B. Du Bois criticized Washington for failing to comprehend that economic power could not be achieved without political power, which was the only way to achieve civil rights.

Above:
A CUDGELLING MATCH, CIRCA 1810
A competition of martial-arts skills and techniques between English and French slaves on the island of Dominica. Artist: A. Brunias

Opposite:
MUSICIANS IN HAVANA, CUBA
Photograph, 1860.

Unbeknownst to the slave-ship captains, the daily dancing and exercise regime likely provided one of the bases for the continuity of African-based expressive culture in the New World. For the rhythms and dances preserved during the Middle Passage became the roots of New World African musics and dances.

Singing, drumming, and dancing resurfaced in new, transformed rhythms and musics in slave communities and societies. The Pan-African synthesis started on the slave ships evolved into even greater syntheses in the Americas. In places where there were heavy concentrations of enslaved Africans from a single ethnic or national group, the music and dances of these peoples would come to dominate the musical and dancing practices of their community. Even in such settings, however, Africans from other ethnic and national groups made their contributions to the developing new cultural form. More typically, Africans from a number of different ethnicities and nationalities created something new out of the cultural and material resources found in their new environment. They built their religious and secular rituals, festivals, and social gatherings on the foundations of songs, dances, and rhythms they invented to cope with and express their New World realities. Neo-African religions—Santería, Shango, Umbanda, Vodou, etc.—all rely on African-based rhythms, musics, and dances. Carnival and adjunkaroo festivals trace their musical and dancing roots to these neo-African traditions. Indeed, most contemporary musical forms and vernacular dances of the Caribbean and the South trace their roots to the musical and dance heritages of their enslaved African ancestors.

In the United States, the dominant forms of contemporary American music and vernacular dance are also derived from America's African-based slave legacy. This has occurred despite the fact that drums, the rhythmic foundation of African music and dance, were outlawed in many slave communities in the United States. When slave "masters" and overseers in the United States discovered that drums could be used as a secret means of communication, they were banned. But African rhythmic sensibility would not die. Nor could it be suppressed. In the place of drums, enslaved Africans in the United States substituted hand clapping, "pattin' juba," and tapping the feet in polyrhythmic cadences to reproduce the complex rhythms of African drumming. Vernacular dances such as jigs, shuffles, breakdowns, shale-downs, and backsteps, as well as the strut, the ring shout, and other religious expressions, were danced to the accompaniment of these drum-less rhythms and to the fiddle, the banjo, bows, gourds, bells, and other hand or feet instruments—all New World African inventions by enslaved Africans. During the

slavery era, enslaved Africans became the musicians of choice for white and
black celebrations and festivities because they were recognized by whites and
blacks as the best musicians in their locales. Ironically, the most frequently
reported occupation of fugitive slaves in New York during the colonial era
was "musician," by a very wide margin. Two indigenous African-American
musical forms—the spiritual and the blues—were created by enslaved
Africans during the slavery era. African-American religious and secular songs
trace their roots to the spirituals and the blues, respectively.

Enslaved African craftsmen and visual artists laid the foundations of the
African-American visual arts tradition during slavery as well. Slave craftsmen
made furniture and other utilitarian objects, some of which carried unique
New World African visual arts expressions. Carvers and stone sculptors have
left utilitarian objects and artworks of surprising aesthetic quality.
Quiltmakers fashioned objects of beauty from scraps of cloth, and stone
milliners and tailors were among the nation's pioneer fashion designers.

Enslaved Africans left their cultural stamp on other aspects of American
culture. Southern American speech patterns, for instance, are heavily influenced by the language patterns invented by enslaved Africans. Southern
cuisine and "soul food" are nearly synonymous. Both are African-American
cuisines from the slavery era. Sermons, oratory, and other forms of oral literature in the African-American vernacular idiom, including contemporary
rap, trace their roots to genres developed by enslaved Africans during slavery.

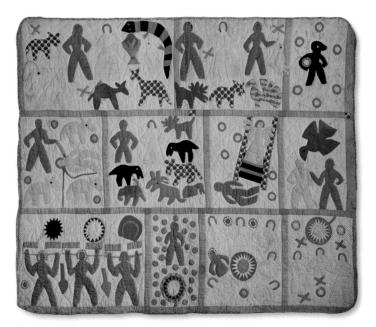

Ira Aldridge

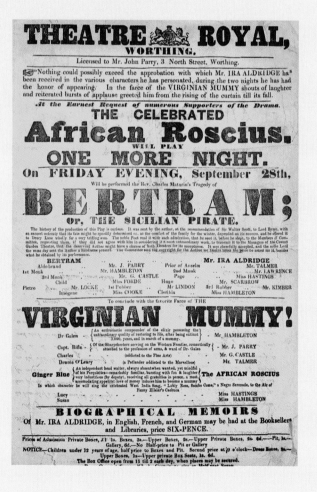

Expressions of serious black culture found it difficult to survive in the United States during the 19th century. Theaters closed, black actors were threatened, and playwrights such as Louisiana-born Victor Séjour (1817-1874), the son of a prosperous free black man and a free mixed-race woman, immigrated to Paris, where he had a successful career.

The African Grove Theatre in the Greenwich Village region of New York City was the first professional black theater company in the United States. Founded in 1821, the theater staged Shakespearean and other classical plays. In 1822 the African Grove was shut down by police after white rowdies disrupted a Saturday night performance. Despite an order by police to keep the theater closed, the Grove's actors tried to stage **Richard III** the following Monday night but were arrested on stage minutes after the play began. The Grove reopened but closed forever in 1823.

Born in New York City, **IRA ALDRIDGE** (circa 1807-1867) attended the African Free School and received early acting experience at the African Grove Theatre. His father, a minister, sent him to the University of Glasgow to continue his schooling, but instead Aldridge left college to become an actor in London. Billed as a native of Senegal and dubbed "The African Roscius" when he made his debut in the role of Othello at the Theatre Royal in Covent Garden in 1833, he played many Shakespearean parts including Shylock in the **Merchant of Venice.** Acclaimed as one of the greatest Shakespearean tragediens ever, Aldridge settled in Europe and never returned to the United States. He died in Poland in 1867.

Pianist **THOMAS "BLIND TOM" WIGGINS BETHUNE** (1849-1908), born a slave near Columbus, Georgia, could play a variety of musical styles, including classical compositions, which he had only to hear once to be able to play. Slaves with musical talent meant

Left: **"THE CELEBRATED AFRICAN ROSCIUS,"**
LONDON, CIRCA 1840
Broadside for a performance by Ira Aldridge.

income for their owners and so Tom was "hired out" regularly from the age of nine. During the Civil War, Tom's talents were used at fund-raising concerts to raise money for the southern cause. After the war, Tom, who earned virtually nothing from his concerts, was showcased as a musical phenomenon, but frequently as a freakish novelty. He was a musical genius, and his concerts regularly included top musicians who performed the most difficult selections in their repertoires, which Tom followed with precise piano renditions.

Left: **"TOM, MUSICAL PRODIGY," NEW YORK, 1868**
Broadside for performance by pianist Blind Tom.

FROM CAKE WALKS TO CONCERT HALLS

William Henry Lane "Master Juba"

America's most popular entertainment form in the 19th century was the minstrel show. Minstrelsy usually featured white performers, in blackface, mimicking blacks. Black entertainers (dancers, singers, and musicians) were regular performers in minstrel shows, which required them to blacken their faces for "authenticity." In the 1800s few blacks were able to succeed as "serious" performers, but they still influenced American music and dance forms greatly during the century.

WILLIAM HENRY LANE (1825-1852) is the best known and most influential African-American dancer of the pre- and post-Civil War era. Popular with black and white audiences, Lane appeared regularly at Irish dance halls, where he was acclaimed for his ability to dance the Irish jig. Lane improvised greatly on the jig, creating American tap dancing. Author Charles Dickens is believed to have observed Lane first-hand when he wrote about spending an evening at a New York City dance hall, watching the "greatest dancer known." Master Juba, Lane's honorific name, is considered a derivation of giouba, a West African or Yoruba dance. Juba was danced in a circle, always moving counterclockwise, with other dancers "patting juba"—clapping rhythmically.

Haverly's Genuine Colored Minstrels, circa 1878

Minnie Tate. *Maggie Porter.* *Thos. Rutling.* *Eliza Walker.*
Isaac Dickerson. *Jennie Jackson.* *Ella Sheppard.* *Benj. M. Holmes.*
Green Evans.

The New Jubilee Singers who left Fisk University, October 6, 1871.

FISK JUBILEE SINGERS, 1871 (above). Founded at Fisk University in 1867, the Fisk Jubilee Singers popularized Negro spirituals among white audiences in the United States and Europe. Their national and international tours raised money for the university. (Left to right) Minnie Tate, Green Evans, Isaac Dickerson, Jennie Jackson, Maggie Porter, Ella Sheppard, Thomas Rutling, Benjamin M. Holmes, and Eliza Walker.

ELIZABETH TAYLOR GREENFIELD, circa 1824-1876 (right). Born a slave in Natchez, Mississippi, Greenfield was known for her remarkable range and flexibility. Critics favorably compared the soprano to European singers Jenny Lind and Teresa Parodi. In 1853 Frederick Douglass criticized Greenfield for performing before an all-white audience of 4,000 people at a New York City concert. In turn, Greenfield, the first nationally and internationally famous African-American singer, gave a benefit performance for the city's Colored Orphan Asylum and the Home of Aged Colored Persons.

179

THE PHENOMENON OF SOUL IN AFRICAN-AMERICAN MUSIC

AMIRI BARAKA

Ultimately, all African-American music springs from African music, which was both religious and secular. African-American music, as it develops from African, then African with elements found in the diaspora, then African-American, develops as both religious and secular. And the secular obviously would be more ubiquitous. But the church was almost the only black institution allowed to develop in any depth early in black people's lives in the West, and that institution was a vehicle for the development and circulation of the religious music.

The work song was primarily secular, but there were always similar musical and emotional elements in both aspects of black musical culture. Plus there are deep references to a spiritual life in all of the music. The religious music might yearn for a crossing into a new life, a raising of this life onto "higher ground," an ultimate salvation of the person and their soul and freedom from this wearying slavery world.

The secular, too, would speak of a time when "the sun's gonna shine in my backdoor someday" or shout that things won't always be like this, meaning that there will be a time of more money, more love, more self-fulfillment—that such a time will surely come. There is a harsh critical realism, but also a final optimism.

There were church shouts and field and juke-joint shouts and hollers and yells. But perhaps the church hollers were a little more intense, the shouters and screamers seeking literally to transport themselves away from here into that other world merely by the energy of their screamed belief. Spirit Possession in the black church is not a variable; unless one is possessed by the spirit (at some time) one was not really there for serious business, and this goes back into the mists of the ancient past. One only had religion if one literally was possessed by it; one had to, as my grandmother said, "Get happy" or religion was mighty shallow. My wife's grandmother, a member of one of the small sanctified churches, told her that if people didn't get happy, "they didn't love God."

W. E. B. Du Bois, in *The Souls of Black Folk,* says of the black church, its music, and its characteristic spirit possession, "The Music of Negro religion is that plaintive rhythmic melody, with its touching minor cadences, which, despite caricature and defilement, still remains the most original and beautiful expression of human life and longing yet born on American soil. Sprung from the African forests, where its counterpart can still be heard, it was adapted, changed, and intensified by the tragic soul-life of the slave, until, under the stress of law and whip, it became the only true expression of a people's sorrow, despair and hope.

"Finally the Frenzy or 'Shouting,' when the Spirit of the Lord passed by, and, seizing the devotee, made him mad with supernatural joy, was the last essential of Negro religion and the one more devoutly believed in than all the rest. It varied in expression from the silent rapt countenance or the low murmur and moan to the mad abandon of physical fervor—stamping, shrieking, and shouting, the rushing to and fro and wild waving of arms, the weeping and laughing, the vision and the trance. All this is nothing new in the world, but old as religion, a Delphi and Endor. And so firm a hold did it have on the Negro, that many generations firmly believed that without this visible manifestation of the God there could be no true communion with the Invisible."

Although the frenzy or spirit possession was the most important aspect of black religion, Du Bois says that it was one of three elements: "Three things characterized the religion of the slave—the Preacher, the Music and the Frenzy." In the black musician, even of a secular bent, all three of these aspects of the black church are combined! The form of much black music is in the call-and-response structure of preacher and congregation, plus the response of the audience in nightclub or concert hall is much like that of the fervent congregation. There are "Yes, sirs!" and "Yehs" and even some

"Amens" shouted back at the musician, not just the silent murmurs of the Western concertgoer.

The black religious form expands past religion and historically permeates the entire culture, whether manifested through the African-American nation's poets or its football running backs who, after scoring a touchdown, might do a Holy Roller wiggle and leap in the end zone to express their joy! Certainly in that vehement fervor we hear in black song there is the ancient spirit possession remanifesting itself, whether the singer is Aretha Franklin, Shirley Caesar, Little Jimmy Rushing, James Brown, Stevie Wonder, Joe Le Wilson, or Sarah Vaughan.

What brought the concept of Soul so forcefully into the present was its use in the fifties. The history of African-American music reflects the general lives and history of the African-American people. It is the music of a people suffering oppression and racism, but its beauty exists despite this tragic fact. National oppression consists of robbery, denial of rights, and exploitation. These are expressed in most facets of black life. So that in the music, for instance, as the black masses created their various styles, the chance to benefit materially by their own creations, whether individually or collectively, was (and is) severely limited. Slavery itself was certainly the most extreme limitation a human could experience. The discrimination, the segregation, the continuing racism that followed offered little better. African-American music was, and is, considered a "raw material" that could be appropriated and casually exploited with little or no compensation for its creators.

From its earliest appearance, and even today, the initial response of the larger society's social and aesthetic establishment was that the music, like black people themselves, was degraded, degenerate, and savage. But when one wants to reconstruct a portrait of this country at any time in the 20th century, one must go to black music to express the North American environment. The tendency to dismiss the music as "primitive," on one hand, and to imitate it and utilize it for profit, on the other, are the twin social relationships of the establishment's ethic. And at each stylistic plateau of African-American music, not only will we find much grand talk about how hopeless black music is, we will at the same time find a great deal of imitation, appropriation, and exploitation of it going on.

For the traditional music, there was the "Dixieland"; the big bands spawned by Fletcher Henderson and brought to perfection by Duke Ellington had a commercial counterpart called Swing. For Bebop the counterpart was "Cool." In all of these cases, what was being done was that once the black style had surfaced and become popular, corporate interests would concoct a watered down version of that style played mainly by white performers and aimed mainly at the white middle class.

The fifties was a period of marked reaction in the United States. These were the years of McCarthyism and the insanity of its anti-Communist witch hunts. It was the period of the Korean War, the Cold War, and President Eisenhower, whom intellectuals ridiculed. So that it was really a part of the whole character of the fifties that the decade would produce a music that would "cover" the hot rebellious music of the forties. Fifties' "Cool" was almost the exact opposite of the forties' innovative and provocative Bebop.

The fact that in the fifties the regular rhythms and grinning American countenances of Dave Brubeck, Chet Baker, Shorty Rogers, Gerry Mulligan, and others should be used to cover the harsh and jagged uncompromising sounds and alien black faces of Charlie Parker, Thelonius Monk, Bud Powell, Dizzy Gillespie is part of the whole period of American reaction which also saw Langston Hughes, W. E. B. Du Bois, Paul Robeson dragged before the House Un-American Activities Committee and threatened for being black and radical, while Richard Wright was driven from these shores to France in permanent exile.

But at each threatened swallowing of the people and their music by the corporate villains, there is a resistance, an adjustment, a restating of the people's fundamental values. So that the Dixieland reaction only forced new expressions like the big band; and the anti-swing "Swing" bands produced small groups opposed to their dullness who produced the music called Bebop! The cool reaction brought a sharp countermotion from the creators of the people's music. Cool threatened to starch and flatten the life out of black music, to replace its organic swing and the hotness created there from mechanical lifelessness in which blues was all but eliminated and improvisation, the lifeblood of the music, replaced by mediocre charts.

What breathed new life into the music in the fifties was the arrival (or re-arrival) of Soul. People like Horace Silver, Art Blakey and his Jazz Messengers, Max Roach and Clifford Brown and their classic groups, Sonny Rollins, and some others went back to the wellspring of black music, the African-American church. Particularly this was true of Silver and Blakey and the others in those groups that called forth the epithet "funky" to describe their music as well as "soul." Which meant that what they had created was basic, elemental, and so strong it could be perceived in extramusical ways, as "funk" was once used to describe a heavy odor associated with sex. The blues, added to the traditional spirituals, produced what was called gospel music; now the gospel tradition and even earlier churchy modes laid on the modern jazz sounds produced a soul music. An antidote for the antidote!

Musicians like Max Roach, Clifford Brown, and Sonny Rollins—who at one time during the fifties were the featured players in one of the most influential and important groups in the music, the Clifford Brown-Max Roach Quintet featuring Sonny Rollins—not only were aware of the influx of church-oriented rhythms but went to the immediate past and brought the bebop impulse into the new decade with all its fire and feeling. The music they made was called by critics hard bop, and together with the soul-music influence revitalized black music in the fifties, uncovering it from under the suffocating "Cool." What Soul also signified was the element of ethnicity that is the national consciousness of the black players. In the face of the watered-down Cool, which eradicated any African-American identity to the music, Soul and Funk meant also not just feeling, but a feeling connected most directly with the African-American experience.

Part of the exploitation of African-American music has always been to appropriate it as some anonymous expression in the world, and not as the creation, primarily, of the African-American people. How can a people be oppressed as "worthless" if they are actually creators? Which is why the fiction of black music's "anonymity" continues. So that the terms soul and soulful also refer to the music's origins as an African-American cultural projection, finally, no matter the players. Because what is being expressed in the music, in its original and most striking forms and content, is the existence of a particular people and their description of the world.

This element of national consciousness is also very apparent in the most sophisticated players and composers, whether Duke Ellington or in the fifties' Sonny Rollins's *Freedom Suite,* which proposes to make a social statement about liberation while at the same time being a musical example of that liberation from hackneyed Tin Pan Alley forms of commercial music.

Max Roach's *We Insist: Freedom Now,* which included the voice of traditional musical Africa as well as the voice and social statement of contemporary Africa and the link between the African freedom struggle and the African-American struggle, shows how high this national consciousness can be brought. So that what is soulful expresses not a metaphysical freedom, as the surfaces of the old spirituals did, but speaks to the liberation of a living people (just as many of the old spirituals did, laying on more symbol as well).

What Max Roach, Clifford Brown, and Sonny Rollins were playing in the fifties points directly to what was called Avant-Garde in the sixties, given a special urgency by the key figure of the period, John Coltrane. Coltrane is so important because he was the musician who brought together a wide expression of musical influences—black church, rhythm and blues, big band, bebop, hard bop—to create the most evocative and influential sound and style of his time. Coltrane is the essence of the Soul-playing black jazz musician. His playing is about and induces spirit possession in a way as fundamental as the church. Later, he even pointed directly to the forms of spirit possession older than the African-American church; he pointed to Africa and the East, and to the ancient divinities that still inhabit the consciousness of humanity.

"Trane" also spoke to black national consciousness, not only as a soulful player, but by the very forms he used that opposed commercial music in the extreme and spoke of African and African-American spiritual and cultural reality. Frequently, in fact, Trane is linked to the black leader Malcolm X, not only because they were contemporaries, but the fire and vision and rage heard in Trane's music seemed to complement the violent truths of the great Malcolm! And that is another element not included in the perception of what is soulful: that it be an expression of truth and the fullest expression of that truth in all its naked blinding beauty and power. Malcolm told it like it was, and Trane played it like it was—hot and illuminating!

Many of the players influenced by Trane and the earlier boppers, who were called the Avant-Garde, e.g., Ornette Coleman, Albert Ayler, Eric Dolphy, Cecil Taylor, created a "new music" that was also, at its most expressive, a soul music, i.e., a music of deep emotion and widening consciousness, a music that seemed as essential as life itself. But by the late seventies the corporate hosts had descended again to counterfeit feeling and fill their pockets. This time there were two aspects to their desouling process. On one hand they created a music much like fifties Cool but that utilized the bass rhythms associated with rhythm and blues, with a cool top or melodic line and instrumentation, so that what was arrived at was called Fusion. In the late seventies and early eighties this was a commercial music that was all but ubiquitous even in many of the places one might look for legitimate and soulful jazz. Fusion, in the main, had no soul because it smelled of commercial dilution and money tricks.

It must be recognized, however, that what makes black music soulful is that it is an authentic reflection of those people who created it, and an organic expression of their lives. If we spoke of Russian music or Spanish music or Gypsy music or French music or German music, etc., people would have less problem understanding that one aspect of those musics would be a quality that expressed with some precision real-life elements of those musics' originators. Beethoven is certainly a universal genius, but one clear identification of his creation is as German Music. There is a cultural, historic, and social reference in the music that is quite German. But that is the music's particularity, and nothing can be universal unless it also expresses the particular. "The universal is a collection of all the particulars!"

In the most authentic African-American music, the quality of soulfulness comes from the elements Du Bois mentioned that characterized the black church, but these elements go back much further than even the existence of an African-American people, back into the mists of the African past. First there is the Preacher quality, or the direct communication with the audience (congregation) and its necessary response. Second, the intense emotionalism (the shouting or "getting happy" element) in the music, and as a result of the communication, in the listener. And then there is the conceptualizing of the music as an ultimate concern, as in the religion. As black musicians say "The Music" with a seriousness that is as reverent as any religious focus.

With these "religious" qualities there is also a more generalized commit-ment to feeling, like the intense emotionalism or frenzy of the church. There is also that commitment and will to *be* the truth, as well as to express it. And with that, the national consciousness of the most sophisticated musi-cians that they are African Americans as are their creations, and this can be taken as expression, definition, or in many cases in so twisted a world, defense! But hopefully, also, development.

To be soulful is to be in touch with the truth and to be able to express it, openly and naturally and without the shallow artifice of commerce. And finally, it is the truth of a particular national experience that, in its most important expressions, is clearly international and accessible as art and reve-lation to the world.

THE JUBILEE CAKEWALK

JUBILEE meant biblical emancipation, and for newly freed African Americans, their freedom was to be celebrated with jubilation—and jubilee singers and dancers. From its plantation origins, the cakewalk was an elegant and dignified part of the black minstrel variety program. The cakewalk ended every show, as the best dancers competed for prizes, with the winner determined by audience applause. On plantations the prize was a freshly baked cake—as in the expression "taking the cake." Some historians believe the cakewalk derived from black servants mocking the ballroom dances held by the white plantation elite. However, they adapted it so well that they enjoyed the dance as their own creation.

Photograph, circa 1890.

JUBILEE

Proclamation of EMANCIPATION

Whereas On the 22nd day of September, in the year of our Lord 1862 a PROCLAMATION was issued by the PRESIDENT OF THE UNITED STATES containing among other things the following, to wit: That on first day of January in the year of our Lord one thousand eight hundred and sixty three, all PERSONS held as SLAVES within any state or designated part of a state, the people whereof shall then be in Rebellion against the United States, shall be thenceforth and forever FREE and the Executive Government of the United States including the Military and Naval authority thereof, will recognize and maintain the freedom of such persons and will do no act or acts to repress such persons or any of them in any effort they may make for their actual freedom, that the executive WILL on the first day of January aforesaid issue a Proclamation designating the states and parts of states if any in which the people therein respectively shall then be in Rebellion against the United States, and the fact that any state or the people thereof shall on that day be in good faith represented in the Congress of the United States by members chosen thereto at elections wherein a majority of the qualified voters of such states shall have participated, shall in the absence of strong countervailing testimony, be deemed conclusive evidence that such state and the people thereof are not in Rebellion against the UNITED STATES.

Now therefore I ABRAHAM LINCOLN PRESIDENT OF THE UNITED STATES BY VIRTUE OF THE POWER VESTED IN ME AS COMMANDER IN CHIEF OF THE ARMY AND NAVY in a time of actual armed Rebellion against the authority of the Government of the United States, as a fit and necessary WAR MEASURE for suppressing said Rebellion, do, on this first day of January, in the year of our Lord One Thousand Eight Hundred and Sixty Three, and in accordance with my purpose so to do, publicly proclaimed for the full period of one hundred days from the date of the first above mentioned order, designate as the states and parts of states therein, the people whereof respectively are this day in Rebellion against the United States, the following to wit: Arkansas, Texas and Louisiana, (except the parishes St. Bernard, Plaquemine, Jefferson, St. John, St. Charles, St. James, Ascension, Assumption, Terrebonne, La Fourche, St. Mary, St. Martin and Orleans, including the City of New Orleans,) Mississippi, Alabama, Florida, Georgia, South Carolina, North Carolina and Virginia, (except the forty eight counties designated as West Virginia, and also the Counties of Berkley, Accomac, Northampton, Elizabeth City, York, Princess Anne and Norfolk, including the Cities of Norfolk and Portsmouth) which excepted parts are for the present left precisely as if this Proclamation were not issued: and by virtue of the power and for the purpose aforesaid, I do ORDER AND DECLARE that all persons held as SLAVES within designated States, or parts of States ARE and henceforward shall be Free and that the Executive Government of the United States, including the military and naval authorities thereof, will recognize and maintain the freedom of the said persons, & I hereby enjoin upon the people so declared to be free, to abstain from all violence, unless in necessary self-defense, and I recommend to them that in all cases where allowed they labor faithfully for reasonable wages, and I further declare and make known that such persons of suitable condition, will be received into the Armed Service of the United States, to garrison forts, positions, stations and other places & to man vessels of all sorts in said service. And upon this sincerely believed to be an act of JUSTICE warranted by the CONSTITUTION

CHAPTER 9

A New World in This Wilderness

The struggle for black freedom in the United States has a long history. It dates from the settling of the first enslaved Africans in today's South Carolina in 1526. Over the next 340- odd years, through revolts, petitions, acts of sabotage, labor, flight, rebellion, military service, and other acts of self-liberation, enslaved Africans pursued their persistent quest for freedom.

In 1860 Abraham Lincoln was elected President of the United States. His Republican Party platform opposed the expansion of slavery into the American West. Southern leaders decided to secede from the Union and establish their own nation, the Confederate States of America, in order to preserve and protect slavery. On April 12, 1861, the new Confederate Army attacked and captured Fort Sumter, a U.S. government fortress in Charleston, South Carolina. The shots fired on Fort Sumter started the American Civil War. They also sounded the death knell of legal slavery in the United States.

By the 1860s slavery had been abolished in most countries and colonies in the Americas. Indeed, by the 1860s slavery, which had existed in virtually every human society since the beginning of modern civilization, had been declared morally and socially reprehensible. All of the states north of the Mason-Dixon Line had abolished it. Haiti waged a successful slave revolution to destroy it, and except for Cuba, Brazil, and Puerto Rico, all of the islands and nations of the Americas had abolished slavery except the United States.

The U.S. Census of 1860 indicated that only 448,070 of the 4.4 million people of African descent living in the United States were free. Over 3.9 million were still held in bondage throughout the American South. Within hours of the arrival of the first Union troops on Southern battlefields, enslaved Africans made themselves fugitives from injustice. These self-emancipating acts were in the tradition of the maroons and fugitives who had stolen themselves and run away from slave systems and slave labor. Throughout the war years, they used the disruptions of the war to strike out—as individuals, families, and communities—for their freedom.

Above:

"WE'S FREE," NEEDLEPOINT, CIRCA 1866

A personal expression of freedom and joy made by a former slave shortly after the Civil War

Opposite:

EMANCIPATION PROCLAMATION

Designed by A. Kidder, New York City, 1864

Preceding pages:

BAPTISM, NEWPORT NEWS, VIRGINIA

A woman joins the mass baptism of the United House of Prayer for All People, held each year in the James River.

Following pages:

FUGITIVE AFRICAN AMERICANS, AUGUST 1862, RAPPAHANNOCK RIVER, VIRGINIA

When the Union soldiers entered the South, thousands of slaves fled to Union camps. Called "contraband of war," many fugitives greatly aided the Union war effort with their labor.

Abraham Lincoln steadfastly claimed that he was fighting the Civil War to preserve the Union. Black Americans—slave and free—maintained that the future of the nation and the war could not be secured without abolishing slavery. According to Frederick Douglass, "The war now being waged in this land is a war for and against slavery, and it can never be effectively put down till one or the other of these vital forces is completely destroyed."

Not until he authorized the Emancipation Proclamation in 1862 did Abraham Lincoln come to this realization. On September 22, 1862, he issued his Preliminary Emancipation Proclamation, which declared that on January 1, 1863, he would free all slaves held in bondage by states in rebellion against the United States. This marked the first time in American history that the U.S. government had gone on record in favor of abolishing slavery anywhere. As limited as it was as a legal instrument of abolition, the Emancipation Proclamation did authorize, for the first time, the recruitment of black soldiers. It also signaled to black Americans—slave and free—that the Civil War was a war for or against slavery.

Lincoln followed through on his threat, and on January 1, 1863, the Emancipation Proclamation was signed into law. Enslaved Africans in the Confederate states became instant fugitives—contrabands of war, according to the U.S. government. They exercised their legal freedom by abandoning plantations and taking up residence with the Union Army. Some volunteered for military service. Others worked and provided support for the Union forces. By the end of the war more than 200,000 blacks had served in the military services, and 38,000 had lost their lives in battle.

The Civil War and the passage of the 13th Amendment ended slavery in the United States. The Emancipation Proclamation placed the U.S. government on the side of freedom and helped make the Declaration of Independence and the Constitution real for African Americans.

CONTRABAND

Only a few weeks after the Civil War broke out in April 1861, many slaves escaped across the Union line and declared their freedom. In May U.S. Maj. Gen. Benjamin F. Butler refused to honor a Confederate colonel's request for the return of slaves who had fled across the Union line at Fortress Monroe, Virginia. Butler termed the runaways "contraband of war" and put them to work at the camp.

Many Northern regiments gave refuge to fugitives and refused to give them up despite orders to do so, in accordance with U.S. policy. Though several thousand men, women, and children fled slavery during the Civil War, their legal status remained ambiguous until issuance of the Emancipation Proclamation.

Left: Group of contrabands at the headquarters of General Lafayett, May 1862.

PUBLISHED BY THE SUPERVISORY COMMITTEE FOR RECRUITING COLORED REGIMENTS 1210 CHESTNUT ST. PHILADELPHIA.

FROM SLAVES TO SOLDIERS

From the opening days of the Civil War, thousands of free blacks and fugitive slaves volunteered for the Union Army, only to be denied service by President Lincoln, who argued that the war was being fought to restore the Union, not to end slavery. Believing the war would be short-lived and the Union successfully restored, Lincoln prohibited black soldiers from the Union ranks to avoid angering his own border states, Delaware, Kentucky, Maryland, and Missouri, where slavery was still protected by the Constitution.

However, as the war lengthened and worsened, President Lincoln's slavery policy or strategy changed profoundly. On September 22, 1862, he issued a preliminary Emancipation Proclamation, which effectively warned that if the South did not end its rebellion within 100 days (by January 1, 1863) all slaves in the South were to be freed. The edict also permitted former slaves and Northern blacks to enter the armed services. Volunteers from South Carolina, Tennessee, and Massachusetts filled the first authorized black regiments. By the end of the Civil War, about 179,000 black men (10 percent of the Union Army) served as soldiers in the U.S. Army and another 19,000 served in the Navy. On April 9, 1865, at the Appomattox Court House, 12 "colored" regiments, or about 3,500 black soldiers, stood guard outside with white Union soldiers as Gen. Robert E. Lee surrendered to Gen. Ulysses S. Grant.

(continued on next page). . .

Opposite, top: **"COME AND JOIN US BROTHERS,"** 1863
A Union recruiting poster for black troops during the Civil War

Opposite, bottom: Seven "contraband" dressed in old Union uniforms, 1864, Virginia

*Black Union Soldier's Cap,
Cloth and leather, 1864*

Flag, 26th U.S.C.T.

About 40,000 black soldiers died during the war—30,000 of infection or disease. Black soldiers served in artillery and infantry and performed support functions that sustained the army. Black carpenters, blacksmiths, cooks, laborers, teamsters, nurses, scouts, spies, steamboat pilots, and surgeons also contributed to the war cause. There were nearly 80 black commissioned officers. Black women, who were not formally allowed to join the Army, served as nurses, spies, and scouts, including Harriet Tubman (circa 1820-1913), the Army's most famous scout.

26TH UNITED STATES COLORED TROOPS Organized on February 27, 1864, the 26th U.S.C.T. infantry regiment trained for six weeks before breaking camp on Riker's Island and boarding the steamship **Warrior** for Beaufort, South Carolina. Like white soldiers, the men of the United States Colored Troops experienced combat and deprivations in the field, including hunger, payless months, and debilitating diseases. There were no nonwhite officers among the 26th U.S.C.T., and only its black chaplains received officer status. Mustered out of the service in August 1865, the regiment lost 5 officers and 140 enlisted men during the war, as a result of combat and disease.

Above: **"MUSTERED OUT"** *Colored Volunteers at Little Rock, Arkansas.* Harper's Weekly, *May 19, 1866.*
Opposite, top: **RETURN OF COMPANY I** *100th Regiment, United States Colored Infantry, for the month of April 1865, Tennessee.*
Opposite, bottom: **STORMING FORT WAGNER** *Charge of the 54th Massachusetts Colored Regiment, July 18, 1863.*

PRESENT.				ABSENT.					PRESENT AND ABSENT.			ALTERATIONS SINCE LAST MONTHLY RETURN.				MEMORANDA.
COMMISSIONED OFFICERS.	ENLISTED MEN.		COMMISSIONED OFFICERS.		ENLISTED MEN.		WHERE.		COMMISSIONED OFFICERS.	ENLISTED MEN.			GAIN.	LOSS.		HORSES.	PIECES ARTILLERY.

ENLISTED MEN on "Extra or Daily duty," accounted for by name.
(The *specific* kind of such duty to be carefully stated.)

ABSENT ENLISTED MEN, accounted for by name.
(The *nature, commencement, period,* and *place,* of absence to be invariably stated.)

NOTE 1.—*Actions*, in which the company, or any portion of it, has been engaged; *scouts, marches, changes of stations, &c., everything of interest,* relating to the *discipline, efficiency,* or *service* of the company, will be minutely and carefully noted, with date, place, distance marched, &c., &c.

NOTE 2.—The name and rank of the officers and soldiers *killed* or *wounded,* in action, with date and place, will be accurately noted.

NOTE 3.—One copy of this return will be transmitted, on the first of each month, to the Adjutant at Regimental Headquarters. Blanks will be supplied to companies from the Adjutant General's Office, and their receipt must be promptly acknowledged.

THE EMANCIPATION PROCLAMATION:
AN ACT OF JUSTICE

JOHN HOPE FRANKLIN

Thursday, January 1, 1863, was a bright, crisp day in the nation's capital. The previous day had been a strenuous one for President Lincoln, but New Year's Day was to be even more strenuous. So he rose early. There was much to do, not the least of which was to put the finishing touches on the Emancipation Proclamation. At 10:45 the document was brought to the White House by Secretary of State William Seward. The President signed it, but he noticed an error in the superscription. It read, "In testimony whereof I have hereunto set my name and caused the seal of the United States to be affixed." The President had never used that form in proclamations, always preferring to say "In testimony whereof I have hereunto set my hand…" He asked Seward to make the correction, and the formal signing would be made on the corrected copy.

The traditional New Year's Day reception at the White House began that morning at eleven o'clock. Members of the Cabinet and the diplomatic corps were among the first to arrive. Officers of the Army and Navy arrived in a body at half past eleven. The public was admitted at noon, and then Seward and his son Frederick, the Assistant Secretary of State, returned with the corrected draft. The rigid laws of etiquette held the President to his duty for three hours, as his secretaries Nicholay and Hay observed. "Had necessity required it, he could of course have left such mere social occupation at any moment," they pointed out, "but the President saw no occasion for precipitancy. On the other hand, he probably deemed it wise that the completion of this momentous executive act should be attended by every circumstance of deliberation."

After the guests departed, the President went upstairs to his study for the signing in the presence of a few friends. No Cabinet meeting was called, and no attempt was made to have a ceremony. Later, Lincoln told F. B. Carpenter, the artist, that as he took up the pen to sign the paper, his hand shook so violently that he could not write. "I could not for a moment control my arm. I paused, and a superstitious feeling came over me which made me hesitate…. In a moment I remembered that I had been shaking hands for hours with several hundred people, and hence a very simple explanation of the trembling and shaking of my arm." With a hearty laugh at his own thoughts, the President proceeded to sign the Emancipation Proclamation. Just before he affixed his name to the document, he said, "I never, in my life, felt more certain that I was doing right than I do in signing this paper."

When I made my first serious study of this document, several copies of the December 30 draft were in existence. The copies of Cabinet officers Edward Bates, Francis Blair, William Seward, and Salmon P. Chase were in the Library of Congress. The draft that the President worked with on December 31 and the morning of New Year's Day is considered the final manuscript draft. The principal parts of the text are written in the President's hand. The two paragraphs from the Preliminary Proclamation of September 22, 1862, were clipped from a printed copy and pasted on the President's draft, "merely to save writing." The superscription and the final closing are in the hand of a clerk in the Department of State. Later in the year, Lincoln presented his copy to the ladies in charge of the Northwestern Fair in Chicago. He told them that he had some desire to retain the paper, "but if it shall contribute to the relief and comfort of the soldiers, that will be better," he said most graciously. Thomas Bryan purchased it and presented it to the Soldiers' Home in Chicago, of which he was president. The home was destroyed in the Great Chicago Fire of 1871. Fortunately, four photographic copies of the original had been made. The official engrossed document is in the National Archives and follows Lincoln's original copy.

It is worth observing that there was no mention, in the final draft, of Lincoln's pet schemes of compensation and colonization, which were in the Preliminary Proclamation of September 22, 1862. Perhaps Lincoln was about to give up on such impracticable propositions. In the Preliminary

Proclamation, the President had said that he would declare slaves in designated territories "thenceforward, and forever free." In the final draft of January 1, 1863, he was content to say that they "are, and henceforward shall be free." Nothing had been said in the preliminary draft about the use of blacks as soldiers. In the summer of 1862 the Confiscation Act had authorized the President to use blacks in any way he saw fit, and there had been some limited use of them in noncombat activities. In stating in the Proclamation that former slaves were to be received into the armed services, the President believed that he was using congressional authority to strike a mighty blow against the Confederacy.

It was late afternoon before the Proclamation was ready for transmission to the press and others. Earlier drafts had been available, and some papers, including the *Washington Evening Star* had used those drafts, but it was at about 8 p.m. on January 1 that the transmission of the text over the telegraph wires actually began.

Young Edward Rosewater, scarcely 20 years old, had an exciting New Year's Day. He was a mere telegraph operator in the War Department, but he knew the President and had gone to the White House reception earlier that day and had greeted him. When the President made his regular call at the telegraph office that evening, young Rosewater was on duty and was more excited than ever. He greeted the President and went back to his work. Lincoln walked over to see what Rosewater was sending out. It was the Emancipation Proclamation! If Rosewater was excited, the President seemed the picture of relaxation. After watching the young operator for a while, the President went over to the desk of Tom Eckert, the chief telegraph operator in the War Department, sat in his favorite chair, where he had written most of the Preliminary Proclamation the previous summer, and gave his feet the proper elevation. For him, it was the end of a long, busy, but perfect day.

For many others in various parts of the country, the day was just beginning, for the celebrations were not considered official until word was received that the President had actually signed the Proclamation. The slaves of the District of Columbia did not have to wait, however, for back in April 1862, the Congress had passed a law setting them free. Even so, they joined in the widespread celebrations on New Year's Day. At Israel Bethel Church, the Reverend Henry McNeal Turner went out and secured a copy of the *Washington Evening Star* that carried the text of the Proclamation. Back at the church, Turner waved the newspaper from the pulpit and began to read the document. This was the signal for unrestrained celebration characterized by men squealing, women fainting, dogs barking, and whites and blacks shaking hands. The Washington celebrations continued far into the night. In the Navy Yard, cannon began to roar and continued for some time.

In New York the news of the Proclamation was received with mixed feelings. Blacks looked and felt happy, one reporter said, while abolitionists "looked glum and grumbled … that the proclamation was only given on account of military necessity." Within a week, however, there were several large celebrations in which abolitionists took part. At Plymouth Church in Brooklyn, the celebrated Henry Ward Beecher preached a commemorative sermon to an overflow audience. "The Proclamation may not free a single slave," he declared, "but it gives liberty a moral recognition." There was still another celebration at Cooper Union on January 5. Several speakers, including the veteran abolitionist Lewis Tappan, addressed the overflow audience. Music interspersed the several addresses. Two of the renditions were the "New John Brown Song" and the "Emancipation Hymn."

A veritable galaxy of leading literary figures gathered in the Music Hall in Boston to take notice of the climax of the fight that New England abolitionists had led for more than a generation. Among those present were John Greenleaf Whittier, Henry Wadsworth Longfellow, Oliver Wendell Holmes, Harriet Beecher Stowe, Francis Parkman, and Josiah Quincy. Toward the close of the meeting, Ralph Waldo Emerson read his "Boston Hymn" to the audience. In the evening, a large crowd gathered at Tremont Temple to await the news that the President had signed the Proclamation. Among the speakers were Judge Thomas Russell, Anna Dickinson, Leonard Grimes, William Wells Brown, and Frederick Douglass. Finally, it was announced that "it is coming over the wire," and pandemonium broke out! At midnight, the group had to vacate Tremont Temple, and from there they went to the Twelfth Baptist Church at the invitation of its pastor, Leonard Grimes. Soon the church was packed, and it was almost dawn when the assemblage dispersed. Frederick Douglass pronounced it a "worthy celebration of the first step on the part of the nation in its departure from the thraldom of the ages."

The trenchant observation by Douglass that the Emancipation Proclamation was but the first step could not have been more accurate. Although the presidential decree would not free slaves in areas where the United States could not enforce the Proclamation, it sent a mighty signal both to the slaves and to the Confederacy that enslavement would no longer be tolerated. An important part of that signal was the invitation to the slaves to take up arms and participate in the fight for their own freedom. That more than 185,000 slaves as well as free blacks accepted the invitation indicates that those who had been the victims of thraldom were now among the most enthusiastic freedom fighters.

Meanwhile, no one appreciated better than Lincoln the fact that the Emancipation Proclamation had a quite limited effect in freeing the slaves directly. It should be remembered, however, that in the Proclamation he called emancipation "an act of justice," and in later weeks and months he did everything he could to confirm his view that it was An Act of Justice. And no one was more anxious than Lincoln to take the necessary additional steps to bring about actual freedom. Thus, he proposed that the Republican Party include in its 1864 platform a plank calling for the abolition of slavery by constitutional amendment. When he was "notified" of his renomination, as was the custom in those days, he singled out that plank in the platform calling for constitutional emancipation and pronounced it "a fitting and necessary conclusion to the final success of the Union cause." Early in 1865, when Congress sent the amendment to Lincoln for his signature, he is reported to have said, "This amendment is a King's cure for all the evils. It winds the whole thing up."

Despite the fact that the Proclamation did not emancipate the slaves and surely did not do what the 13th Amendment did in winding things up, it is the Proclamation and not the 13th Amendment that has been remembered and celebrated over the past 130 years. That should not be surprising. Americans seem not to take to celebrating legal documents. The language of such documents is not particularly inspiring, and they are the product of the deliberations of large numbers of people. We celebrate the Declaration of Independence, but not the ratification of the Constitution. Jefferson's words in the Declaration moved the emerging Americans in a way that Madison's committee of style failed to do in the Constitution.

Thus, almost annually—at least for the first hundred years—each New Year's Day was marked in many parts of the country by a grand celebration, replete with brass band, if there was one; an African-American fire company, if there was one; and social, religious, and civic organizations. African Americans of the community would march to the courthouse, some church, or the high school. There, they would assemble to hear the reading of the Emancipation Proclamation, followed by an oration by a prominent person. The speeches varied in character and purpose. Some of them urged African Americans to insist upon equal rights; some of them urged frugality and greater attention to morals; whereas still others urged their listeners to harbor no ill will toward their white brethren.

JOINT RESOLUTION OF THE OF THE UNITED

THIRTY EIGHTH CONGRESS STATES OF AMERICA,

PROPOSING AN AMENDMENT TO THE CONSTITUTION OF THE UNITED STATES,

ABOLISHING SLAVERY.

" Resolved by the

SENATE and HOUSE of REPRESENTATIVES

of the UNITED STATES of AMERICA in CONGRESS assembled,

(two thirds of both houses concurring,) that the following Article be proposed to the Legislatures of the several States as an AMENDMENT to the CONSTITUTION of the UNITED STATES; which, when ratified by three fourths of said Legislatures, shall be valid to all intents and purposes as a part of the said Constitution, namely: **ARTICLE XIII.**

Section 1. NEITHER SLAVERY NOR INVOLUNTARY SERVITUDE except as a punishment for crime whereof the party shall have been duly convicted SHALL EXIST WITHIN THE UNITED STATES or any place subject to their jurisdiction.

Passed in the Senate April 8th 1864.

M. Forney Secretary of the Senate.

H. Hamlin

Vice President of the United States & President of the Senate.

Section 2. Congress shall have power to enforce this Article by appropriate Legislation."

Passed on the House of Representatives, January 31st 1865.

Edw. McPherson Clerk of the House.

Schuyler Colfax

Speaker of the House of Representatives.

Approved Feb. 1st 1865. *A. Lincoln*

THOSE WHO VOTED AYE UPON THE PASSAGE OF THE ABOVE JOINT RESOLUTION WERE THE FOLLOWING SENATORS AND REPRESENTATIVES.

H S Lane
Jas W. Grimes
James Dixon
W. T. Willey
L. F. S. Foster
L. M. Morrill
H. B. Anthony
P. G. Van Winkle
Dan Clark
John Conness
J. Collamer
John P. Hale
E. D. Morgan
Jno. C. Ten Eyck
Jn. Sherman
Wm Sprague
Ira Harris
Henry Wilson
Charles Sumner
J. H. Lane
Reverdy Johnson
Solomon Foot
S. C. Pomeroy
Tim o. Howe
Jas. Harlan
M. S. Wilkinson
B. Gratz Brown
J. Chandler
Aly. Ramsey
Edgar Cowan
J. B. Henderson
B. F. Wade
J. W. Nesmith
J. M. Howard

A. Myers, Pa.
J. M. Ashley Ohio
Ignatius Donnelly
J. G. Blaine
M. Russell Thayer
J. F. Farnsworth
Thaddeus Stevens
D. F. Littlejohn
Henry L. Deming
J. C. Sloan
Augustus Frank
H. Winter Davis
John H. Hubbard
Wm. B. Allison
J. F. Driggs
Green W. Scofield
Sidney Perham
E. C. Ingersoll
J. W. Patterson N.H.
John D. Baldwin, Mass.
Wm. H. Miller Penn.
D. Morris N.Y.
Tho. T. Davis N.Y.
Nathan F. Dixon R.I.
H. L. Dawes Mass.
C. R. Eckley
Joseph Bailey
Francis Thomas
James S. Rollins of Mo.
Sempronius H. Boyd
Cornelius Cole
F. C. Beaman
Fred. A. Pike Maine.
N. B. Smithers Del.
S. F. Miller N.Y.
James S. Gale
John Ganson
Samuel Knox

Godlove S. Orth
E. H. Rollins N.H.
J. B. Grinnell
A. W. Hubbard
F. Kellogg
Wm. Higby
H. Price Iowa
W. B. Washburn
Geo. S. Boutwell
Theodore M. Pomeroy
John H. Starr N.J.
a. c. Wilder
Jno. W. Longyear
J. W. McClurg Mo.
J. Moorhead
Wm. D. Kelley
Amasa Cobb
A. H. Coffroth
Henry T. Blow
Jno. McBride
Jas. M. Marvin
Anson Herrick
James E. English
Austin A. King
Thomas D. Eliot
Alex. H. Rice
Chas. Upson
Wm. Windom
Justin S. Morrill
J. A. Kasson
Schuyler Colfax Ind.
Leonard Myers
D. W. Gooch
John A. Griswold
W. A. Hutchins Ohio
John A. Kasson

Portus Baxter
Oakes Ames Mass
B. G. Odell Ohio
James F. Wilson Iowa
A. W. Clark New York
Jesse O. Norton Ills.
Calvin T. Hulburd N.Y.
Fredk. E. Woodbridge Vt.
R. B. Van Valkenburgh N.Y.
Rob. C. Schenck O.
H. W. Tracy Penna
Henry G. Worthington
Benjn. F. Loan Mo.
James A. Garfield
F. B. Blanchard
Chas. O'Neill
M. F. Odell
Isaac N. Arnold
Edwin H. Webster
Augs. C. Baldwin
Ezra Wheeler
Geo. Yeaman
G. W. Scofield
W. H. Randall
F. W. Kellogg Mich.
John H. Rice
R. P. Spalding
H. A. Nelson Vermont.
Kel. V. Whaley
Jacob B. Blair West Va.
Augustus Brandegee
John B. Alley
Lucien Anderson Ky.
Gilman Marston N.H.
Wm. A. Cresswell
A. W. Allison Penna

FIFTEENTH AMENDMENT CELEBRATION IN BALTIMORE, MAY 19, 1870

ABOLISHING SLAVERY

In 1876 African Americans worried rightly that gains made during the Reconstruction era might rapidly erode, as the presidential election of 1876 signaled the end of Reconstruction. The election between Rutherford B. Hayes and Samuel Tilden was among the most bitterly contested in U.S. history. With Tilden leading in the popular vote, the Republicans negotiated with the Democrats for electoral votes. In exchange for electoral votes and his ultimate Republican victory, Hayes agreed to withdraw federal troops from three southern states—Florida, Louisiana, and South Carolina. Removal of the troops gave Democrats, or southern conservatives, virtually unchallenged control of local and state governments. Termed the Compromise of 1877, the arrangement ushered in the post-Reconstruction period known as Redemption—the return of antebellum social, economic, and political conditions to the South. Black codes or "Jim Crow" laws limiting the civil rights of African Americans followed in states throughout the South.

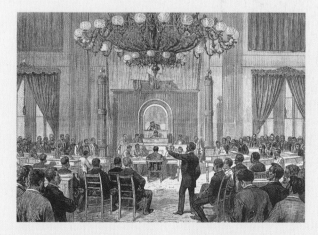

At the Colored National Convention, held at Nashville on April 5, 6, and 7, and May 6, 1876, delegates discussed the social, economic, and political future of African Americans.

Opposite:
THIRTEENTH AMENDMENT, DECEMBER 18, 1865.

EPILOGUE

It is still too soon to write the final chapter on the impact of the slave trade and slavery on the modern world. Although it is true that more than 500 years have passed since the first enslaved Africans were transported to the Americas, the economic, political, social, and cultural impact of their presence and labor, as well as their political and cultural activities, is still resonating within African-descended communities and in the societies and cultures in which they reside. Indeed, in many instances, the most American features of the cultures of the Americas are rooted in the New World African inventions created by enslaved Africans centuries ago. In short, people of African descent—descendants of the 10 million slave captives who survived the Middle Passage—are still vital, at times defining parts of the American political, social, and cultural landscape.

To begin with, there are more than 200 million people of African descent living throughout the Americas. More than 70 million live in Brazil, the largest single importer of enslaved Africans during the slavery era. At the dawning of the 21st century, Brazil has the second largest African-descended population in the world. Only Nigeria has a larger African population.

Descendants of some 450,000 pioneer African immigrants to the United States now number more than 36 million people. Originally concentrated in the rural American South, on tobacco, rice, and cotton plantations, they're now among the most urban of American (U.S.) populations. Every major American city includes significant numbers of people of African descent. And what was, in the 19th century, a southern regional population is now a genuinely national one. There are African-American communities in the Northeast and the Southwest as well as the Mississippi Valley, the Midwest, and the West. African-descended people are found in every state in the union, including Alaska and Hawaii.

Often unknowingly, they carry with them the legacies of the slavery era. Whether it is in the form of the religion they practice, the musics and dances they create and enjoy, the foods they eat, the family rituals they practice,

"WE ARE FAMILY"
Jamaican oral history recalls brave maroons who fled the lowland plantations and hid in the mountains to live in freedom. Their descendants still take their children to a tree in Jamaica's maroon territory and tell them tales about their heroic maroon ancestors.

213

the languages they speak, or the aesthetic principles they embrace, the African-American cultural forms invented by their enslaved African ancestors are in them, in their families, in their communities. These legacies of the slavery era are also found in the so-called mainstream cultures, where Euro-Americans unknowingly have incorporated elements of enslaved African cultural legacies into their language, religion, cuisine, etc. Nowhere is this more prevalent than in southern American culture, but it can also be seen in contemporary urban settings and the American national culture. African-American popular music, for instance, is America's most distinctive music.

Counted among the more than 36 million people of African descent living in the United States at the beginning of the 21st century are millions who migrated here voluntarily during the 20th century. They came from the islands of the Caribbean, continuing a pattern that began during the slavery era. Descendents of enslaved Africans from Jamaica, Trinidad and Tobago, Barbados, Cuba, Haiti, Puerto Rico, and the Dominican Republic, among others, have all migrated to the United States in great numbers during the 20th century, adding to the New World African diversity of the African-descended population in the United States. Each one of their unique cultural creations—legacies of the slavery era in the islands—has enriched and reinforced the legacies that trace their origins to the slave and free black communities of the United States. African-descended communities in many parts of the United States are multilingual and multicultural, reflecting the growing presence of the 20th-century immigrants from New World African communities in the Caribbean.

Lesser numbers of New World Africans have come to the United States from South and Central America—Panama, Mexico, Guatemala, Ecuador, Colombia, Venezuela, Peru, Chile, and, of course, Brazil. These Afro-Hispanics and Afro-Portuguese have added their linguistic, religious, and cultural voices to the continually evolving New World African cultural environment in the United States.

One of the most surprising New World African cultural transformations began some 20 years ago and continues to play a major role in defining and revitalizing the African presence in the United States. During the last two decades of the 20th century (1980-2000) about a million continentally born Africans migrated to the United States and settled principally in the nation's urban centers—New York, Washington, D.C., Chicago, Atlanta, Houston, etc. That's almost twice as many continentally born African migrants as those who came during the slavery era. Their impact on traditional African-American and American cultures is just beginning to be felt. In places like Brooklyn and Queens, New York, and Washington, D.C., traditional African businesses are emerging, traditional African religions as well as Islam are being practiced, and traditional African languages are being interwoven into the traditional African-American, New World African, and American discourses. Traditional African aesthetic principles and public rituals have also become part of the African-American and American cultural terrain.

All of this is to say that the African cultural presence is apparently here to stay in America. So are the cultural legacies of the slavery era in the United States. Far from being mere victims of slavery, racism, and cultural oppression in the United States and the Americas, enslaved Africans and their descendants have been active, creative, thinking human beings who made their own histories and cultures during slavery and continue to do so today. Wherever we look on the American political, cultural, social, or economic landscape in the 21st century, people of African descent are also involved in shaping America's history, culture, and destiny. They are worthy carriers of the legacy of their enslaved African forebears who found a way to make a way out of no way, and made it possible for African Americans not only to survive the worst that slavery had to offer but to prevail.

Howard Dodson
Director, Schomburg Center for Research in Black Culture

ACKNOWLEDGMENTS

"Lest We Forget: The Triumph Over Slavery," the Schomburg Center's inaugural 75th anniversary exhibition, opened to the public on Saturday, June 3, 2000, in the Center's main exhibition hall and Latimer/Edison Gallery. Containing more than 400 items—books, documents, newspapers, artworks, and artifacts drawn principally from the Center's collection, the exhibition was the most comprehensive one ever produced on the slave trade and slavery in this country. It was extended twice due to public demand and attracted thousands of visitors during its run. The continuing enthusiasm highlighted the need to document this important exhibition and to make its content available to a wider audience. What began as an exhibition evolved, after a lot of work by a great many people, into *Jubilee: The Emergence of African-American Culture*, and we couldn't be more thrilled.

I am especially grateful to The Carl and Lily Pforzheimer Foundation, Inc., for its financial support. I also extend warm thanks to Annette Gordon-Reed, Amiri Baraka, Gail Lumet Buckley, Henry Louis Gates, Jr., Gayraud S. Wilmore, and John Hope Franklin, *Jubilee*'s talented contributors, who have shared their knowledge and insight with us.

I am indebted to all the lenders who allowed us to include their artifacts in the exhibition and book: Rod Brown; Velma Clay; The Drain Collection, Walterboro, South Carolina; Tom Feelings; Nana Kweku Egyir Gyepi III; Charles Lilly; Eugene Peters; Sample Noel Pittman; Eugene and Adele Redd; Vivian Rittner; and The Stirling Historical Society, Greenport, New York.

I gratefully recognize the knowledgeable Schomburg Center library staff, whose early work helped make both projects possible. Special thanks to Diana Lachatanere, curator of the Manuscripts, Archives and Rare Books Division; Mary Yearwood, curator of the Photographs and Prints Division; James Briggs Murray, curator of the Moving Image and Recorded Sound Division; Tammi Lawson of the Art and Artifacts Division; and Roberta Yancy, head of Public Affairs and Development. Thanks also to Schomburg

Center Public Affairs and Development staffers Christopher Moore, research coordinator; and Jacqueline Dowdell, editor; and to Karen Van Westering, Publications Director, The New York Public Library, for her early support and enthusiasm.

In addition to Schomburg Center staff, I am grateful to a number of professionals who worked on this project in both its incarnations. Manu Sassoonian photographed some 400- plus images from the exhibition for the book; J. R. Sanders Design designed and installed the "Lest We Forget" exhibition; and Ken McFarlin produced innumerable print pieces related to both projects.

Finally, my thanks to the talented individuals at the National Geographic Society who helped ferry the project from exhibition to book form, especially Lisa Lytton for her patience, guidance, and editorial vision. Thanks to Nina Hoffman, publisher of the National Geographic Book Division; Kevin Mulroy, editor-in-chief; Rebecca Lescaze for careful text editing; Melanie Doherty, who brought the book to life with her brilliant design; and photo researcher Susan Blair, who worked with the Schomburg Center's indefatigable Christopher Moore to find additional photographs for *Jubilee*.

BIBLIOGRAPHY

INTRODUCTION

Berlin, Ira. *Many Thousands Gone: The First Two Centuries of Slavery In North America.* Cambridge: Belknap Press, 1998.

Berlin, Ira, ed. *Free At Last: A Documentary History of Slavery, Freedom, and the Civil War.* New York: The New Press, 1992.

Eltis, David. *The Rise of African Slavery in the Americas.* Cambridge, England: Cambridge University Press, 2000.

Franklin, John Hope. *From Slavery to Freedom: A History of African Americans.* Boston: McGraw-Hill, 2000.

Gomez, Michael Angelo. *Exchanging Our Country Marks: The Transformation of African Identities in the Colonial and Antebellum South.* Chapel Hill: University of North Carolina Press, 1998.

Hall, Gwendolyn Midlo. *Africans in Colonial Louisiana: The Development of Afro-Creole Culture in the Eighteenth Century.* Baton Rouge: Louisiana State University Press, 1992.

Johnson, Charles. *Africans in America: America's Journey Through Slavery.* New York: Harcourt Brace, 1998.

Lovejoy. Paul E. ed. *Identity in the Shadow of Slavery.* London: Continuum, 2000.

Piersen, William D. *From Africa to America: African American History From the Colonial Era to the Early Republic, 1526-1790.* New York, N.Y.: Twayne, 1996.

Thomas, Velma Maia. *Lest We Forget: The Passage From Africa to Slavery and Emancipation.* New York: Crown, 1997.

Williamson, Joel. *New People: Miscegenation and Mulattoes in the United States.* New York, N.Y.: Free Press, 1980.

TRANSATLANTIC SLAVE TRADE

Cugoano, Ottobah. *Thoughts and Sentiment on the Evil of Slavery: And Other Writings.* New York, N.Y.: Penguin, 1787.

Curtin, Philip D. *The Atlantic Slave Trade: A Census.* Madison: University of Wisconsin Press, 1969.

Doudou Diene, ed. *From Chains to Bonds: The Slave Trade Revisited.* New York, N.Y.: Berghahn Books, 2001.

Eltis, David. *Economic Growth and the Ending of the Transatlantic Slave Trade.* New York, N.Y.: Oxford University Press, 1987.

Eltis, David., and David Richardson, eds. *Routes to Slavery: Direction, Ethnicity, and Mortality in the Transatlantic Slave Trade.* Portland: Frank Cass, 1997.

Equiano, Olaudah. *The Interesting Narrative of the Life of Olaudah Equiano or Gustavus Vassa, the African, Written by Himself.* Edited by Vincent Carretta. New York, N.Y.: Penguin, 1995.

Gates, Henry Louis, Jr., ed. *Pioneers of the Black Atlantic: Five Slave Narratives From the Enlightenment, 1772-1815.* Washington, D.C. : Civitas, 1998.

Inikori, Joseph. *The Atlantic Slave Trade: Effects on Economies, Societies and Peoples in Africa, the Americas, and Europe.* Durham, N.C.: Duke University Press, 1992.

Klein, Herbert S. *The Atlantic Slave Trade.* New York, N.Y.: Cambridge University Press, 1999.

Smith, Venture. *A Narrative of the Life and Adventures of Venture, a Native of Africa, but Resident Above Sixty Years in the United States of America.* Middletown, Conn, 1897.

Thomas, Hugh. *The Slave Trade.* New York, N.Y.: Simon & Schuster, 1997.

AFRICA: THE LONG MARCH

Barry, Boubacar. *Senegambia and the Atlantic Slave Trade.* Cambridge, England: Cambridge University Press, 1998.

Curtin, Philip D., ed. *Africa Remembered: Narratives by West Africans From the Era of the Slave Trade.* Project Heights: Waveland Press, 1997.

Curtin, Philip. *Migration and Mortality in Africa and the Atlantic World, 1700-1900.* Burlington: Ashgate/Variorum, 2001.

Law, Robin., and Paul E. Lovejoy, eds. *The Biography of Mahommah Gardo Baquaqu: His Passage From Slavery to Freedom in Africa and America.* Princeton, N.J.: Markus Wiener Publishers, 2001.

Lovejoy, Paul. *Transformations in Slavery: A History of Slavery in Africa.* Cambridge, England: Cambridge University Press, 1983.

Miller, Joseph C. *Way of Death: Merchant Capitalism and the Angolan Slave Trade, 1730-1830.* Madison: University of Wisconsin Press, 1988.

Miller, Joseph C., and Paul Finkelman, eds. *Macmillan Encyclopedia of World Slavery.* New York, N.Y.: Macmillan Reference, 1998.

THE PRICE OF CHAINS

Berlin, Ira, and Philip D. Morgan, eds. *Cultivation and Culture: Labor and the Shaping of Slave Life in the Americas.* Charlottesville: University Press of Virginia, 1993.

Berlin, Ira, and Philip D. Morgan, eds. *The Slaves' Economy: Independent Production by Slaves in the Americas.* London: Frank Cass, 1991.

Bolster, W. Jeffrey. *Black Jacks: African American Seamen in the Age of Sail.* Cambridge, Mass.: Harvard University Press, 1997.

Curtin, Philip. *The Rise and Fall of the Plantation Complex: Essays in Atlantic History.* New York, N.Y.: Cambridge University Press, 1998.

Klein, Martin A. *Historical Dictionary of Slavery and Abolition.* Lanham: Scarecrow Press, 2002.

Kulikoff, Allan. *Tobacco and Slaves: The Development of Southern Cultures in the Chesapeake, 1680-1800.* Chapel Hill: University of North Carolina Press, 1986.

Littlefield, Daniel. *Rice and Slaves: Ethnicity in the Slave Trade in Colonial South Carolina.* Baton Rouge: Louisiana University Press, 1981.

Solow, Barbara, ed. *Slavery and the Rise of the Atlantic System.* Cambridge, England: Cambridge University Press, 1991.

Wood, Peter H. *Black Majority; Negroes in Colonial South Carolina From 1670 Through the Stono Rebellion.* New York, N.Y.: Knopf, 1974.

ROUTES TO FREEDOM

Finkelman, Paul, ed. *Rebellions, Resistance, and Runaways Within the Slave South.* New York, N.Y.: Garland, 1989.

Franklin, John Hope, and Loren Schweninger. *Runaway Slaves: Rebels on the Plantation, 1790-1860.* New York, N.Y.: Oxford University Press, 1999.

Hodges, Graham Russell., and Brown, Alan Edward, eds. *"Pretends to Be Free": Runaway Slave Advertisements From Colonial and Revolutionary New York and New Jersey.* New York, N.Y.: Garland Pub., 1994.

Landers, Jane. *Black Society in Spanish Florida.* Urbana: University of Illinois Press, 1999.

Berlin, Ira, Joseph P. Reidy, and Leslie S. Rowland, eds. *The Black Military Experience.* Cambridge, England: Cambridge University Press, 1983.

Berlin, Ira ed. *Slaves No More: Three Essays on Emancipation and the Civil War.* Cambridge, England: Cambridge University Press, 1992.

Geggus, David P., ed. *The Impact of the Haitian Revolution in the Atlantic World.* Columbia: University of South Carolina, 2001.

Pearson, Edward A., ed. *Designs Against Charleston: the Trial Record of the Denmark Vesey Slave Conspiracy of 1822.* Chapel Hill: University of North Carolina Press, 1999.

Bogger, Tommy. *Free Blacks in Norfolk, Virginia, 1790-1860: The Darker Side of Freedom.* Charlottesville: University Press of Virginia, 1997.

Phillips, Christopher. *Freedom's Port: The African American Community of Baltimore, 1790-1860.* Urbana: University of Illinois Press, 1997.

Walker, Lois, and Susan R. Silvermann. *A Documented History of Gullah Jack Pritchard and the Denmark Vesey Slave Insurrection of 1822.* Lewiston: E. Mellen Press, 2000

A BOTTOMLESS VITALITY

Berlin, Ira, and Leslie S. Rowland, eds. *Families and Freedom: A Documentary History of African-American Kinship in the Civil War Era.* New York, N.Y.: New Press, 1997. New York, N.Y.: Pantheon Books, 1976.

Blassingame, John W. *The Slave Community: Plantation Life in the Antebellum South.* New York, N.Y.: Oxford University Press, 1979.

Frankel, Noralee. *Freedom's Women: Black Women and Families in Civil War Era Mississippi.* Bloomington: Indiana University Press, 1999.

Genevose, Eugene. *Roll, Jordan, Roll: The World the Slaves Made.* New York, N.Y.: Random House, 1974.

Gutman, Herbert George. *The Black Family in Slavery and Freedom, 1750-1925.*

Horton James Oliver, and Lois E. Horton. *In Hope of Liberty: Culture, Community, and Protest Among Northern Free Blacks, 1700-1860.* New York, N.Y.: Oxford University Press, 1997.

Morgan, Philip D. *Slave Counterpoint: Black Culture in the Eighteenth Century Chesapeake and Lowcountry.* Chapel Hill: University of North Carolina Press, 1998.

Piersen, William D. *Black Yankees: The Development of an Afro-American Subculture in Eighteenth-Century New England.* Amherst: University of Massachusetts Press, 1988.

White, Deborah Gray. *Ar'n't I A Woman? Female Slaves in the Plantation South.* New York, N.Y.: Norton, 1985.

A GLORY OVER EVERYTHING

Angell, Stephen W. and Anthony B. Pinn, eds. *Social Protest Thought in the African Methodist Episcopal Church, 1862-1939.* Knoxville: University of Tennessee Press, 2000.

Cornelius, Janet Duitsman. *Slave Missions and the Black Church in the Antebellum South.* Columbia: University of South Carolina Press, 1999.

Diouf, Sylviane A. *Servants of Allah: African Muslims Enslaved in the Americas.* New York: New York University Press, 1998.

Fulop, Timothy E., and Albert J. Raboteau, eds. *African-American Religion: Interpretive Essays in History and Culture.* New York, N.Y.: Routledge, 1997.

Murphy, Larry G. ed. *Down by the Riverside: Readings in African American Religion.* New York: New York University Press, 2000.

Raboteau, Albert J. *African-American Religion Canaan Land: A Religious History of African Americans.* New York, N.Y.: Oxford University Press, 2001.

Sernett, Milton C. ed. *African American Religious History: A Documentary Witness.* Durham, N.C.: Duke University Press, 1999.

Whelchel, L. H. *Hell Without Fire: Conversion in Slave Religion.* Nashville, Tenn.: Abingdon Press, 2002.

BONDS UNLOOSED AND BROKEN

Andrews, William L. *To Tell a Story: The First Century of Afro-American Autobiography, 1760-1865.* Urbana: University of Illinois Press, 1986.

Blassingame, John, ed. *Slave Testimony: Two Centuries of Letters, Speeches, Interviews, and Autobiographies.* Baton Rouge: Louisiana State University Press, 1977.

Cornelius, Janet Duitsman. *When I Can Read My Title Clear: Literacy, Slavery, and Religion in the Antebellum South.* Columbia: University of South Carolina Press, 1991.

Douglass, Frederick. *Narrative of the Life of Frederick Douglass, an American Slave.* New York, N.Y.: St. Martin's Press, 1993.

Fitts, Leroy and Charles T. Davis. *The Slave's Narrative.* New York, N.Y.: Oxford University Press, 1985.

Jacobs, Harriet Ann. *Incidents in the Life of a Slave Girl.* New York, N.Y.: Penguin. 2000.

Richard Newman, Patrick Rael, and Philip Lapsansky, eds. *Pamphlets of Protest: An Anthology of Early African-American Protest Literature, 1790-1860.* New York, N.Y.: Routledge, 2001.
Wheatley, Phillis. *Memoir and Poems of Phillis Wheatley, a Native African and a Slave.* Boston: Geo. W. Light, 1834.

THE SACRED FIRE

Abbington, James. *Let Mt. Zion Rejoice!: Music in the African American Church.* Valley Forge. Pa.: Judson Press, 2001.

Brown, Fahamisha Patricia. *Performing the Word: African American Poetry as Vernacular Culture.* New Brwick, N.J.: Rutgers University Press, 1999.

Conyers, James L. Jr., ed. *African American Jazz and Rap: Social and Philosophical Examinations of Black Expressive Behavior.* Jefferson: McFarland, 2001.

Gates, Henry Louis, Jr., and Cornel West. *The African-American Century: How Black Americans Have Shaped Our Country.* New York : Free Press, 2000.

Malone, Jacqui. *Steppin' on the Blues: The Visible Rhythms of African American Dance.* Urbana: University Of Illinois Press, 1996.

Piersen, William D. *Black Legacy: America's Hidden Heritage.* Amherst: University of Massachusetts Press, 1993.

Stuckey, Sterling. *Going Through The Storm: The Influence Of African American Art In History.* New York, N.Y.: Oxford University Press, 1994.

Vlach, John Michael. *The Afro-American Tradition in Decorative Arts.* Cleveland: Cleveland Museum of Art, 1978.

White, Shane, and Graham White. *Stylin': African American Expressive Culture From Its Beginnings to the Zoot Suit.* Ithaca, N.Y.: Cornell University Press, 1998.

Ward, Andrew. *Dark Midnight When I Rise: The Story of the Jubilee Singers, Who Introduced the World to the Music of Black America.* New York, N.Y.: Farrar, Straus and Giroux, 2000.

Wilder, Craig Steven. *In the Company of Black Men: The African Influence on African American Culture in New York City.* New York: New York University Press, 2001.

Boldface indicates illustrations.

CHAPTER TITLE SOURCES

CHAPTER 2: THE PRICE OF CHAINS

"Is life so dear or peace so sweet as to be purchased at the price of chains and slavery? Forbid it, Almighty God! I know not what course others may take, but as for me, give me liberty, or give me death!"

PATRICK HENRY

Speech in the Virginia Convention, March, 1775.

CHAPTER 4: A BOTTOMLESS VITALITY

"We were here before the mighty words of the Declaration of Independence were etched across the pages of history. Our forebears labored without wages. They made cotton "king." And yet out of a bottomless vitality, they continued to thrive and develop. If the cruelties of slavery could not stop us, the opposition we now face will surely fail."

MARTIN LUTHER KING, JR.

Letter, April 1963, from Birmingham Jail, Alabama.

CHAPTER 5: A GLORY OVER EVERYTHING

"I looked at my hands, to see if I was de same person now I was free. Dere was such a glory ober eberything, de sun came like gold trou de trees, and ober de fields, and I felt like I was in heaven."

HARRIET TUBMAN

As quoted in Harriet, the Moses of Her People, *by Sarah Bradford (1869).*

CHAPTER 6: BONDS UNLOOSED AND BROKEN

"Slavery is but half abolished, emancipation is but half completed, while millions of freemen with votes in their hands are left without education. Justice to them, the welfare of the States in which they live, the safety of the whole Republic, the dignity of the elective franchise,—all alike demand that the still remaining bonds of ignorance shall be unloosed and broken, and the minds as well as the bodies of the emancipated go free."

ROBERT CHARLES WINTHROP

Yorktown Oration, 1881.

CHAPTER 7: THE SACRED FIRE

O black and unknown bards of long ago,
How came your lips to touch the sacred fire?
How, in your darkness, did you come to know
The power and beauty of the minstrels' lyre?
Who first from midst his bonds lifted his eyes?
Who first from out the still watch, lone and long,
Feeling the ancient faith of prophets rise
Within his dark-kept soul, burst into song?

JAMES WELDON JOHNSON,

"O Black and Unknown Bards"

CHAPTER 8: A NEW WORLD IN THIS WILDERNESS

Fit gravefellows you are for Lincoln, Brown
And Douglass and Toussaint. . . all whose rapt eyes
Fashioned a new world in this wilderness.
American earth is richer for your bones;
Our hearts beat prouder for the blood we inherit.

DUDLEY RANDALL

Poetry of Black America, The; Anthology of the 20th Century. *Arnold Adoff, ed. (1973) Harper & Row.*

THE SCHOMBURG CENTER FOR RESEARCH IN BLACK CULTURE

The Schomburg Center for Research in Black Culture, a research unit of The New York Public Library, is generally recognized as one of the leading institutions of its kind in the world. A cultural center as well as a repository, this Harlem-based modern research library also sponsors a wide array of interpretive programs, including exhibitions, scholarly and public forums, and cultural performances.

The Center's collections number over 5 million items, including over 3.5 million manuscript items, 170,000 books, and 750,000 photographs. Rich collections of periodicals, posters, art objects, films, videotapes, audio recordings, and memorabilia are also counted among these holdings. Five collection divisions provide state-of-the-art storage, preservation, and access environments for its unique resources: General Research and Reference; Manuscripts, Archives and Rare Books; Photographs and Prints; Moving Image and Recorded Sound; and Art and Artifacts.

The Schomburg Center complex, a 75,000 square foot, three-building facility, also houses the 340-seat Langston Hughes Auditorium and the 75-seat American Negro Theater, as well as an exhibition hall and a gallery. The Center currently sponsors more than 60 public programs annually that involve virtually every segment of the population that has an interest in its resources. They provide opportunities for community leaders, schoolchildren, senior citizens, scholars, and artists to meet and engage each other in reflection, discussion, and celebration.

For more than seventy-five years the Schomburg Center has collected, preserved, and provided access to materials documenting black life, and promoted the study and interpretation of black history and culture. For information about Schomburg Center research services and programs and Schomburg Society membership, call or write: The Schomburg Center for Research in Black Culture, 515 Malcolm X Boulevard, New York, New York 10037, (212) 491-2200. Visit the Schomburg Center online at: www.schomburgcenter.org.

PUBLISHED BY THE
NATIONAL GEOGRAPHIC SOCIETY

John M. Fahey, Jr., *President and Chief*
Executive Officer
Gilbert M. Grosvenor, *Chairman of the Board*
Nina D. Hoffman, *Executive Vice President*

PREPARED BY THE BOOK DIVISION

Kevin Mulroy, *Vice President and*
Editor-in-Chief
Charles Kogod, *Illustrations Director*
Marianne R. Koszorus, *Design Director*

STAFF FOR THIS BOOK

Lisa Lytton, *Editor*
Rebecca Lescaze, *Text Editor*
Jackie Dowdell, Schomburg, *Text Editor*
Christopher Moore, Schomburg, *Writer*
Melanie Doherty Design, *Design*
Susan Blair, *Picture Editor*
Meredith Wilcox, *Illustrations Assistant*
Britt Griswold, *Production*
Carl Mehler, *Director of Maps*
NG Maps, *Map Edit, Research, and Production*
Gary Colbert, *Production Director*
Ric Wain, *Production Project Manager*

MANUFACTURING AND QUALITY CONTROL

Christopher A. Liedel, *Chief Financial Officer*
Phillip L. Schlosser, *Managing Director*
Vincent P. Ryan, *Manager*

ESSAY CREDITS

Excerpted from "The Phenomenon of Soul in
African-American Music" in *The Music:*
Reflections on Jazz and Blues by Amiri and Amina
Baraka, © 1987 by Amiri Baraka. Published by
William Morrow and Company, Inc.

The essay by John Hope Franklin is based on a talk
he gave at the National Archives, January 4,
1993, on the occasion of the 150th anniversary
of the signing of the Emancipation
Proclamation.

Excerpted from *The Signifying Monkey: A Theory of*
African-American Literary Criticism by Henry
Louis Gates, Jr., © 1988 by Henry Louis Gates,
Jr. Used by permission of Oxford University
Press, Inc.

Excerpted from "The Religion of the Slave," in
Black Religion and Black Radicalism: An
Interpretation of the Religious History of African
Americans, 3rd edition by Gayraud S. Wilmore,
© 1998 by Gayraud S. Wilmore. Used by
permission of Orbis Books.

PICTURE CREDITS
ABBREVIATIONS:
(t) top, (m) middle, (b) bottom, (l) left, (r) right

A&A: Art and Artifacts Division, Schomburg
Center for Research in Black Culture, The New
York Public Library
Drain: Drain Collection, Walterboro, South
Carolina
GR&R: General Research and Reference
Division, Schomburg Center for Research in
Black Culture, The New York Public Library
LOC: Library of Congress
MARB: Manuscripts, Archives and Rare Books
Division, Schomburg Center for Research in
Black Culture, The New York Public Library
NARA: National Archives and Records
Administration, Northeast Region, New York
NYPL: Manuscripts and Archives Division,
Humanities and Social Sciences Library, The New
York Public Library
P&P: Photographs and Prints Division,
Schomburg Center for Research in Black
Culture, The New York Public Library
Pittman: Sample Noel Pittman Collection
Redd: Eugene and Adele H. Redd Collection

Cover and Endsheets: Drain; P&P.
Front matter, Foreword, and Introduction
1 A&A. **2-3** New Hampshire Historical Society.
6-7 Chicago Historical Society, #ICHi-28567.
8 P&P. **10** Frank Driggs Collection. **12** A&A., ©
Gwendolyn Knight Lawrence, courtesy of the Jacob
and Gwendolyn Lawrence Foundation. **17** P&P.
Chapter 1: The Transatlantic Slave Trade
18-19 Maggie Steber. **20** MARB. **23** MARB. **24**
MARB. **26** (*clockwise from top left*) Musée Crozatier,
Le Puy-en-Velay, France/Giraudon, Bridgeman Art
Library; GR&R; GR&R; Victoria & Albert
Museum, London, UK/ Bridgeman Art Library;
Museo Romantico, Madrid, Spain/Bridgeman Art
Library. **27** (*clockwise from top left*) GR&R; Philip
Mould, Historical Portraits Ltd., London,
UK/Bridgeman Art Library; GR&R; GR&R;
GR&R; GR&R; GR&R. **29** Private collection of
Vivian Ritter. **30** (*l*) Pittman; (*r*) Redd. **31** Redd. **32**
Pittman. **33** (*t*) Redd; (*b*) LOC. **34** Pittman. **35**
A&A. **36** (*t*) Pittman; (*b*) A&A. **37** (*all*) Pittman. **38**
(*t*) From the collection
of the James Ford Bell Library, University of
Minnesota; (*b*) Pittman. **39** Drain. **40** Collection of
Nana Kweku Egyir Gyepi III. **41** The Mariners'
Museum, Newport News, VA. **42** P&P; (*overlay*)
NYPL. **43** Drain. **44-45** A&A. **46** Cliché Ville de
Nantes – Musée du Château des ducs de Bretagne.
47 (*all*) Pittman. **48-49** Maggie Steber.
Chapter 2: The Price of Chains
50 P&P; (*overlay*) MARB. **51** MARB. **52** LOC. **53**
(*t*) Drain; (*bl*) Pittman; (*br*) NARA. **54-55** From the
Penn School Collection. Permission granted by
Penn Center, Inc., St. Helena Island, SC. Courtesy
Southern Historical Collection, #P-3615, Wilson
Library, The University of North Carolina at
Chapel Hill. **56** From the Edward Ward Carmack
Papers, #P-1414, Southern Historical Collection,
Wilson Library, The University of North Carolina
at Chapel Hill. **58** (*t*) A&A; (*b*) Drain. **59** LOC. **60**

(*t*) Redd; (*b*) Drain. **61** (*t*) William E. Wilson
Collection, Georgia Historical Society; (*b*) The
Historic New Orleans Collection, accession nos.
1975.93.1 & 1975.93.2. **62-63** P&P. **64** (*t*) A&A;
(*b*) P&P. **66** (*tl*) Pittman; (*tr*) NARA; (*b*) MARB.
Chapter 3: Routes to Freedom
66 MARB. **67** MARB. **68** (*both*) MARB. **69**
MARB. **70** Pittman. **70-71** Drain. **71** Drain. **72** (*t*)
P&P; (*b*) MARB. **73** (*t*) P&P; (*m*) P&P; (*b*) MARB.
74-75 Collection of Velma Clay. **76** P&P. **77**
MARB. **78** (*l*) A&A; (*r*) Chicago Historical Society,
#ICHi-22169. **79** (*l*) P&P; (*r*) MARB. **86-87** LOC.
88 P&P. **89** (*t*) P&P; (*b*) P&P. **90** (*all*) A&A. **91** (*l*)
MARB; (*r*) Pittman. **92** Madison County Historical
Society. **93** (*t*) Massachusetts Historical Society; (*b*)
Pittman. **94** A&A. **95** A&A. **96** LOC. **97** (*l*) MARB;
(*r*) A&A. **98** Pittman. **99** (*t*) P&P; (*b*) MARB.
100-101 Kansas State Historical Society.
Chapter 4: A New People
102-103 Maggie Steber. **104** Museo del Virreinato,
Mexico. **105** MARB. **106** (*both*) A&A. **107** P&P.
108 A&A. **109** (*both*) A&A. **110-111** Collection
of The New-York Historical Society, #46085.
Chapter 5: A Bottomless Vitality
112 P&P. **113** P&P. **114** (*t*) Redd; (*b*) A&A. **115**
A&A. **116** LOC. **117** P&P, Artwork in the
Collection of the Corcoran Gallery of Art. **118**
(*both*) Drain. **119** Gladstone Collection. **120** Eugene
Peters Collection. **121** (*t*) P&P; (*b*) MARB. **122** (*t*)
A&A; (*b*) LOC. **123** (*t*) Redd; (*b*) A&A. **129**
MARB. **130-131** LOC.
Chapter 6: A Glory Over Everything
132 P&P. **133** P&P. **134** From the DeRosset Family
Papers, #P-214/1, Southern Historical Collection,
Wilson Library, The University of North Carolina
at Chapel Hill. **135** (*t*) P&P; (*b*) LOC. **136** (*t*)
MARB; (*b*) MARB. **137** (*both*) P&P. **138** P&P. **139**
(*t*) Doris Ulmann, P&P; (*b*) Charles Lilly, A&A.
148-149 Valentine Richmond History Center.
Chapter 7: Bonds Unloosed and Broken
150 Collection of The New-York Historical
Society, #50815. **151** P&P. **152** MARB. **153** (*t*)
Gladstone Collection; (*b*) P&P. **154** (*t*)
Hulton | Archive by Getty Images; (*b*) P&P. **156**
MARB. **157** (*all*) MARB. **158-159** Lewis Wickes
Hine/CORBIS. **160** (*t*) Pittman; (*b*) P&P. **161** (*t*)
Courtesy of the Moorland-Spingarn Research
Center, Howard University Archives; (*m*) MARB;
(*b*) P&P. **168-169** LOC.
Chapter 8: The Sacred Fire
170 MARB. **171** P&P. **172** A&A. **173** MARB. **174**
(*t*) Photograph of Harriet Powers (American, 1837-
1911), 2 3/16 x 1 1/4 in. (5.5 x 3.2 cm), Courtesy
Museum of Fine Arts, Boston © 2002 Museum of
Fine Arts, Boston; (*b*) Smithsonian Institution,
National Museum of American History. **175** A&A.
176 (*t*) P&P; (*b*) MARB. **177** (*l*) MARB; (*r*) P&P.
178 (*t*) P&P; (*b*) A&A. **179** (*both*) P&P. **188-189**
Culver Pictures. **190-191** David Alan Harvey.
Chapter 9: A New World in This Wilderness
192 New York State Library. **193** Pittman. **194-195**
LOC. **197** (*both*) CORBIS. **198-199** LOC. **200** (*t*)
P&P; (*b*) LOC. **201** (*l*) P&P; (*t*) Pittman; (*b*) New
York State Division of Military and Naval Affairs.
202 P&P. **203** (*t*) MARB; (*b*) A&A. **210** MARB.
211 (*t*) A&A; (*b*) P&P.
Epilogue: 212 Maggie Steber.